A Few Minutes with God

Arlena D. Lee

Bridgeport, Connecticut

Copyright © 2012 by Arlena D. Lee

All rights reserved. No part of this book may be reproduced, copied, stored or transmitted in any form or by any means – graphic, electronic, or mechanical, including photocopying, recording, or information storage and retrieval systems without the prior written permission of Arlena D. Lee or Hope of Vision Publishing except where permitted by law.

HOV Publishing a division of HOV, LLC.
www.hovpub.com
hopeofvision@gmail.com

Cover Design: Hope of Vision Designs
Editor/Proofreader: Phyllis M. Bridges

Write the Author at:
Arlena D. Lee
Email: arlenadlee7@yahoo.com

For more information about special discounts for bulk purchases, please contact Email: arlenadlee7@yahoo.com or hovpub.com.

ISBN 978-0-9852746-8-9
Library of Congress Control Number: 2012945665

10 9 8 7 6 5 4 3 2 1

Printed in the United States of America

Dedication

This book is dedicated to my mother Arlena B. Lee and my sister Julia Y. Lee. They always encourage me in the work of the ministry. They are truly a blessing in my life. I want to also acknowledge my deceased father, Julius Lee, Jr. who was my greatest friend and confidant. Finally and most importantly I want to acknowledge my Lord and Savior Jesus Christ who leads me and guides me in every area of my life. Thanks Lord for this opportunity to Spread the Gospel of Jesus Christ.

Content

7	Introduction
9	My Lord What A Morning
15	The Issue of the Blood
21	Prayers From Our Father
27	The Power of Love
33	A Walk of Love, A Walk of Grace, A Walk of Faith
39	Who's Knocking At Your Door?
45	There's A Gift In Your Womb
51	Guess Who's Coming To Dinner?
57	Have You Caught Any Fish Lately?
63	Tongues of Fire
71	Circumstantial Evidence
79	A Twist of Fate
87	The Nature of Your Inheritance
95	Journey of A Lost Man
99	Sealed With A Kiss
105	Sin, Sin, And More Sin
111	There's No Storm Without Jesus
115	The Formula For Life
121	Here Comes The Bride
127	Prepare For Landing, Destination Heaven
135	About The Author

Introduction

Throughout my ministry, I have been invited to preach on various occasions. This book of sermons is a compilation of my most favorite works. These sermons are intended to inspire, motivate and challenge you to grow in the word of God. In James 2:26 it says, "For as the body without the spirit is dead, so faith without works is dead also." I present to you this book of sermons as a work of my testimony and my personal relationship with Jesus Christ. I am simply like John the Baptist, "The voice of one crying in the wilderness: prepare the way of the Lord; Make His paths straight." Matthew 3:3. I am simply the Lord's servant.

My Lord What A Morning

Psalm 30:1-12/Psalm 30:5

"Weeping may endure for a night, But joy comes in the morning."
(Psalm 30:5 NKJV)

"My Lord What a Morning" is one of the many Negro spirituals I often heard while attending my alma mater, Bethune Cookman University. Many people around the world spend much of their time pursuing happiness. Everybody wants to be happy. According to Strong's Concordance there are 26 verses in the Bible which refer to the word, happy. The Bible says, "Happy is the man that finds wisdom, And the man who gains understanding" (Proverbs 3:13). If you look in the thesaurus, you will find happiness is a synonym for joy and joy is a synonym for happiness. In the secular world, they are recognized as one in the same. Yet, they are not the same from a biblical point of view. David did not say "weeping may endure for a night but happiness comes in the morning." He used the word joy, intentionally. It was no accident that he used this word.

If we define the word happiness from a biblical point of view, happiness eliminates all obstacles. There is no stress, no strain, and no pain. Happiness is not listed as a fruit of the Spirit. To illustrate this point, we can look at everyday situations which serve as an example of happiness. Happiness is getting married and going on your honeymoon. Happiness is celebrating your birthday. Happiness is getting a promotion on your job. The illustrations that I've given cause no stress, no strain, no pain.

On the other hand, there is joy. The definition of joy is that a person has pleasure regardless of his circumstances. Joy is listed in Galatians 5:22 as a fruit of the Spirit. The fruit of the Spirit comes from the unconscious part of us. We do not put them on. They come from the Spirit. This is the personality or character of the Lord Jesus Christ. David tells us, "weeping may endure for a night, But joy comes in the morning" (Psalm 30:5).

Some illustrations of joy are a woman travailing in birth. When you are in labor and your contractions are coming two minutes apart. It is difficult to think about your new born baby until he arrives. His presence brings joy. If you have ever been sick and the Lord has healed your body, that's joy. When you've been in a car accident and you didn't get hurt, that's joy. When you've fasted and prayed and all of your family is born again, that's joy.

Luke 8:43 describes a woman with an issue of blood for twelve years and no doctor could heal her, but when she touched the hem of Jesus' garment she was made whole. That's joy. In Mark 10:46-52, we are told about blind Bartimaeus sitting by the side of the road begging and crying out, "Jesus Son of David, Have mercy on me!" Jesus said to Bartimaeus, "What do you want me to do for you?" Bartimaeus said, "I want to receive my sight." Jesus said to him, "Go your way; your faith has made you well." When Bartimaeus received his sight, he had a sense of great joy.

In the book of John, chapter 11 tells the story of Lazarus' death and how Jesus raised him from the dead. Lazarus' sisters Mary and Martha knew Jesus well, and when Lazarus became ill, they sent for Jesus. He said, "This sickness is not unto death, but for the glory of God, that the Son of God may be glorified through it." Jesus did not go to Lazarus immediately but waited two more days. When he arrived at Bethany, Lazarus had been in the tomb four days. Martha said to Jesus, "Lord, if You had been here, my brother would not have died."

At the tomb, they took the stone away. Jesus said, "Father, I thank You that You have heard Me. And I know that You always hear Me, but because of the people who are standing by I said this, that they may believe that You sent Me." Now when He had said these things, He cried with a loud voice, "Lazarus, come forth!" And he who had died came out bound hand and foot with grave clothes, and his face was wrapped with a cloth. Jesus said to them, "Loose him, and let him go." When Jesus raised Lazarus from the dead there was also great joy.

The greatest joy is that Jesus died on the cross for your sins. The bible says that He laid down his life. He was crucified between two thieves. Because of His death and resurrection we can have eternal life. That's joy.

Paul says in Romans 14:17, "For the kingdom of God is not eating and drinking, but righteousness and peace and joy in the Holy Spirit." When your mind and heart are in submission to Christ as well as the Holy Spirit, you should not be experiencing technical difficulty, but you should be experiencing the joy of the Lord.

Hebrews 12:2 reads, "Looking unto Jesus, the author and finisher of our faith, who for the joy that was set before Him endured the cross, despising the shame, and has sat down at the right hand of the throne of God." Jesus prepared the disciples for his departure. It was Jesus' inner strength that sustained Him on the cross. He had joy even though He was being crucified because He knew that He would rise again and those who received Him would have eternal life.

The joy of the Lord produced in our hearts by the Spirit enables us to fulfill the admonitions found in the scriptures. "Rejoice in the Lord always. Again I will say, rejoice" (Philippians 4:4). Joy is the ability to rejoice and be content in whatsoever state you find yourself and to be able to cope with life's situations and problems.

When the Christians were persecuted, what did they do? They rejoiced. When the Christians were beaten, what did they do? They rejoiced. When the Christians where put in jail, what did they do? They rejoiced. When the Christians were told not to preach, what did they do? They rejoiced. Everything was cause for joy. Can you defeat people like that? The devil can never defeat a person as long as that person is rejoicing in the Lord. That's why "weeping may endure for a night, But joy comes in the morning" (Psalm 30:5). In whatever situation that you are in, the Spirit will enable you to give thanks, rejoice and express the joy of the Lord.

In Psalm 5:3 David said, "My voice You shall hear in the morning, O Lord; In the morning I will direct it to You, And I will look up." The morning or a dawning of a new day is significant because the Bible says that God's mercies are new every morning. The morning brings a new day, a new challenge, a new opportunity to rejoice in the Lord. The Bible also states that, "The joy of the Lord is your strength" (Nehemiah 8:10).

According to scripture, Abraham rose up early in the morning to prepare a burnt offering for the Lord. Moses rose up early in the morning like the Lord commanded him. He went up early in the morning to Mount Sinai. Moses also rose up early in the morning to build an altar. Jesus arose early on the first day of the week. He appeared to Mary Magdalene out of whom he had driven seven demons. Early in the morning all the chief priests and elders of the people came to the decision to put Jesus to death.

Proverbs 8:17 KJV reads, "I love them that love me; and those that seek me early shall find me." David said, "Evening and morning and at noon I will pray, and cry aloud And He shall hear my voice" (Psalm 55:17). He also states, "But I will sing of Your power; Yes, I will sing aloud of Your mercy in the morning. For You have been my defense And refuge in the day of my trouble" (Psalm 59:16-17).

When the night has ended another chapter of your life, when you've lost hope, when you're weeping in the midnight hour, Jesus hears your cry and says, "Fear not, for I am with you." When you've lost your home, when you've lost your job, when you're lonely and need a friend, when your children are disobedient, when you don't know the answer, you need to get your mind off of your circumstances and put your mind on Jesus. You can go to bed and wake up in the morning and shout "MY LORD WHAT A MORNING." You can shout for joy because Jesus is not buried in a grave.

Paul states, "For I am persuaded that neither death nor life, nor angels nor principalities nor powers, nor things present nor things to come, nor height nor depth, nor any other created thing, shall be able to separate us from the love of God which is in Christ Jesus our Lord" (Romans 8:38).

Each and every day you need to rejoice in knowing that Jesus is working on your behalf to make the crooked places straight and to reveal His perfect will to you. Have hope in knowing that Jesus is the answer, and weeping only last through the night but Joy comes in the morning.

THE ISSUE OF THE BLOOD

Luke 8:43-48/Luke 8:43

"And a woman having an issue of blood twelve years, which had spent all her living upon physicians, neither could be healed of any."(Luke 8:43 KJV)

There are many women in the Bible from Genesis to Revelation. Just like the men in the Bible, some were used for good and some were used for evil. It is unfortunate, but we must admit that a woman was instrumental in the fall of man. Even before discussing the fall of man, let us briefly discuss the creation of man. In Genesis 1:27-28, the Bible says:

> "So God created man in his own image, in the image of God created he him; male and female created he them. And God blessed them, and God said unto them, Be fruitful, and multiply, and replenish the earth, and subdue it: and have dominion over the fish of the sea, and over the fowl of the air, and over every living thing that moveth upon the earth."

Then the Bible says in verse 31, "And God saw everything that he had made, and, behold, it was very good."

Let us notice from this scripture that God created male and female in His image. The Bible notes that God blessed *them* not just him, and everything that he made was good. I don't want to focus entirely on Eve, but let us take a look at Eve for a moment to establish the nature of women. Eve was a leader and a follower. Eve had both qualities in that she allowed the serpent to persuade her to eat the fruit from the forbidden tree. Then she gave it to her husband and he ate the fruit also. She was the first to disobey God thereby, opening both of their eyes. Here lies the fall of man.

> The title of this message, "The Issue of the Blood," is taken slightly out of context to reveal the importance of the redeeming blood of Jesus Christ that was shed for all people both male and female. It is not the issue of the blood, but the issue of blood that tainted a woman for twelve years. The Bible records three accounts of this event, in the books of Matthew, Mark and Luke. The Bible says, "And a woman having an issue of blood twelve years, which had spent all of her living upon physicians, neither could be healed of any" (Luke 8:43). Let us focus on three points, her faith, her healing, and the issue of the blood.

The Bible just says that she was a woman. It does not give her name, age, race, or culture. All three of the accounts in the Bible simply say that she was a woman. She was a woman who had a disease or dis-ease, or malfunctions with her body. She was sick and no doctor could heal her body. The Bible tells us that she had been sick for twelve years. You know twelve years is a long time. She spent all of her money, and all of her savings or income on physicians. They could not help her even though she was a desperate woman who needed to be healed. However, there was no cure.

When you are desperate there are numerous things that can happen. You can become more self-centered rather than God centered. There are so many feelings that can encompass you like anger, sadness, and frustration. This woman had been tested for twelve years. And nothing that she did healed her body. The woman's faith was being tested. Many times women suffer through trials and tribulations. Statistics shows that women, even in this modern day world, deal with divorce, single motherhood, teen pregnancy and lower wages. The women of the world know how it feels when their faith is being tested.

There are two things that can happen to your faith when you are desperate. Desperation can either eliminate your faith or elevate your faith. Eliminating your faith is confessing the negative. Now we must remember that there was no New Testament to read when Jesus was on earth. This woman couldn't read Hebrews 11:1 which says, "Now faith is the substance of things hoped for, the evidence of things not seen." She could not read, "For we walk by faith, not by sight" (2Corinthians 5:7). This woman elevated her faith when she heard about Jesus. She didn't care about the large crowd or that she may not get to speak to Him. There was only one thing in her heart, if she could just touch the hem of His garment. The Bible says that when the woman touched the hem of Jesus' garment she was healed immediately. Jesus didn't hesitate to heal her because she was a woman. Jesus met her at the point of her need. Her faith made her whole.

Peter must be examined. Peter can be indignant sometimes. Luke is the only person who records that Peter, along with the others, asked Jesus, "The multitude throng thee and press thee, and sayest thou, 'Who touched me?'"(Luke 8:45). Peter was a typical man, ladies. He challenged Jesus by asking Him if He was sure that someone had touched Him. Peter had a critical spirit. However, Jesus felt someone touched Him. He knew someone touched Him. He said, "I perceive that virtue is gone out of me" (Luke 8:46).

Peter is really saying, "Jesus, how are we supposed to know who touched you when all of these people are standing out here and pressed against you. This is standing room only and you ask, 'Who Touched Me?'" Peter was trying to solve the problem his way.

Now I want to focus on the issue of the blood. You know blood is very important in our daily lives. Our bodies are filled with blood. We check our blood pressure. We go to the lab to give blood, which checks the level of medications in our bodies. In some places, blood tests are needed to get married. Moreover, there is the body and blood of Jesus Christ that is called communion which Christians take in remembrance of Him. Because of the shed blood of Jesus Christ, we can be saved, delivered, and healed. It is interesting to note that this woman had an issue of blood that would eventually bring death. Accepting Jesus Christ, who shed His blood on Calvary's Cross and believing in His resurrection, can eventually bring eternal life. Paul states, "In whom we have redemption through his blood, the forgiveness of sins, according to the riches of his grace" (Ephesians 1:7).

The issue of blood plagued this woman for twelve years. She was made whole because she stood up to the test. She heard that Jesus was a healer. This story represents the healing power of Jesus, the faith of someone in trouble, and the obstacle she overcame to be healed.

If your faith has ever been tested in your life, if you, have ever been at a place in your life when you need to look to the woman with the issue of blood, ask yourself this question: if you can reach out your hand to touch Jesus' garment, would you hear the

A Few Minutes With God

quiet still voice of Jesus saying, "Who Touched Me?" knowing instantly, that you have been made whole.

Prayers From Our Father

Matthew 6:5-15/ Matthew 6:9

"After this manner therefore pray ye: Our Father which art in heaven, Hallowed be thy name." (Matthew 6:9 KJV)

The Model Prayer is not heard as often in today's worship services. In Matthew 6:5-15, Jesus gives us some instructions on how to pray, where to pray and in what manner to pray. Prayer is a sacred trust between you and the Father. That's why the Model Prayer begins by saying, "Our Father which art in heaven" (Matthew 6:9).

My earthly father passed away many years ago. The year was 1988. And he was fifty-five years old. I remember him today because he would have been seventy-five years old on his birthday March 30th. When my father was living and he felt that I needed to be disciplined, he would always have a little talk with me. My mother and he always agreed on how they would discipline my sister and me. And If I asked my mother something, she would always say, "I have to discuss it with your father." I used to call these discussions board meetings. They were on one accord when making decisions about us. What you say to your child, and how you say it, is very important in building their self-esteem.

A synonym for discipline is training. The Bible says, "Train up a child in the way he should go: and when he is old he will not depart from it" (Proverbs 22:6). The word "train" has many definitions. According to *dictionary.com,* train means "to develop or form the habits, thoughts, or behavior of (a child or other person) by discipline and instructions." In other words, it's not just anything goes! There must be rules and boundaries that aid in the development of children in order for them to become mature and well disciplined adults. However, it was the training from my parents that helped me in many areas of my life.

Proverbs 13:1 NKJV says, "a wise son heeds his father's instruction, But a scoffer does not listen to rebuke." A scoffer is a person who mocks. Notice that Solomon who wrote the book of Proverbs, speaks to the son in particular, rather that the daughter. Proverbs 13:24 NKJV says, "He who spares his rod hates his son, but he who loves him disciplines him promptly." You may ask, "Why is God focusing on the boys?" Well, if you remember correctly, boys will become men and fathers of their household. Therefore, it is critical if you have a son or a daughter, you should pray for them every day and the Spirit will intercede on your behalf.

Disciplining children must be consistent, but loving. You should take the time to allow them to think for themselves. It is like steering a boat and you are the anchor. This is the way your heavenly father disciplines us. Sometimes it is through trials and tribulations that we become more aware of Him.

In Luke 11, the disciples ask Jesus to teach them to pray. He prayed the Model Prayer which is the Lord's Prayer in Matthew and Luke. Jesus teaches the disciples the Lord's Prayer. In Matthew 6: 9-13 KJV Jesus says:

> After this manner therefore pray ye: 'Our Father which art in heaven. Hallowed be thy name. Thy

kingdom come. Thy will be done in earth, as it is in heaven. Give us this day our daily bread and forgive us our debts, as we forgive our debtors. And lead us not into temptation but deliver us from evil: For thine is the kingdom, and the power, and the glory, forever, Amen.'

This is the Lord's Prayer:

Now let us go back to Matthew 6:5-9 KJV. Jesus says: And when thou prayest, thou shalt not be as the hypocrites are: for they love to pray standing in the synagogues and in the corners of the streets, that they may be seen of men. Verily I say unto you, They have their reward. But thou, when thou prayest, enter into thy closet, and when thou hast shut thy door, pray to thy Father which is in secret; and thy Father which seeth in secret shall reward thee openly. But when ye pray, use not vain repetitions, as the heathen do: for they think that they shall be heard for their much speaking. Be not ye therefore like unto them: for your Father knoweth what things ye have need of, before ye ask him.

Now let's focus on Matthew 6 verses 14 and 15. Jesus says, "For if ye forgive men their trespasses, your heavenly Father will also forgive you: But if ye forgive not men their trespasses, neither will your Father forgive your trespasses." These are the secrets of prayer that we often overlook. Get in your closet and then go to the Father who is in heaven with your thanksgivings, your petitions, and your supplications.

In Luke 11, after teaching the disciples the Lord's Prayer, Jesus used the illustration of someone who comes to a friend's house at midnight. Beginning at verse 5, Jesus says:

> And he said unto them, Which of you shall have a friend, and shall go unto him at midnight, and say unto him, Friend, lend me three loaves; For a friend of mine in his journey is come to me, and I have nothing to set before him? And he from within shall answer and say, Trouble me not: the door is now shut, and my children are with me in bed; I cannot rise and give thee. I say unto you, Though he will not rise and give him, because he is his friend, yet because of his importunity he will rise and give him as many as he needeth.

Again in Luke 11: 9-13 Jesus continues teaching his thoughts on prayer in reference to asking, seeking, and knocking. He begins by saying:

> And I say unto you, ask, and it shall be given you; seek, and ye shall find; knock, and it shall be opened unto you. For every one that asketh receiveth; and he that seeketh findeth; and to him that knocketh it shall be opened. If a son shall ask bread of any of you that is a father, will he give him a stone? Or if he ask a fish, will he for a fish give him a serpent? Or if he shall ask an egg, will he offer him a scorpion? If ye then, being evil, know how to give good gifts unto

> your children: how much more shall your heavenly Father give the Holy Spirit to them that ask him?

It is apparent in both cases: the friend coming to someone's house at midnight and Jesus using the illustration which asks the question "How much more shall your heavenly Father give the Holy Spirit to them that ask him?" (Luke 11:13). Jesus makes you think about the significance of our Father.

Jesus says:

> Let not your heart be troubled: ye believe in God, believe also in me. In my Father's house are many mansions: if it were not so, I would have told you, I go to prepare a place for you. And if I go and prepare a place for you, I will come again, and receive you unto my-self; that where I am, there ye may be also. And whither I go ye know, and the way ye know.

> Thomas said unto him, "Lord, we know not whither thou goest; and how can we know the way?" Jesus saith unto him, "I am the way, the truth and the life: no man cometh unto the Father, but by me" (John 14:1-6 KJV).

It was on the cross that Jesus, hanging along with two criminals, was crucified on Calvary. One criminal hung on the right and one on the left. Then Jesus said speaking to His enemies "Father, forgive them; for they know not what they do" (Luke 23:34 KJV). Even in the midst of dying on the cross, Jesus had compassion and a forgiving heart. He fulfilled His purpose and you must fulfill your purpose. Jesus taught the disciples to say, "Our

Father which art in heaven" (Matthew 6:9). If your earthly Father is not present in your life, whether he is deceased or you do not have a good relationship with him, today, I ask you to consider my Father, who is our Father who is in heaven. I'm reminded of a hymn that states, "Faith of our fathers, holy faith we will be true to thee till death." Remember the Prayers from our Father, remember the Lord's Prayer which is the Model Prayer.

The Power of Love

Matthew 22:34-40/ Matthew 22:37

"Jesus said to him, 'You shall love the Lord your God with all your heart, with all your soul, and with all your mind.'"
(Matthew 22:37 NKJV)

Valentine's Day will be celebrated in a few days. What makes Valentine's Day so special is that it is for those people who are in love, or suppose to be in love, with their spouses or significant others. The stores have already started to sell cards and candy and they have cards for every family member and friend.

I find it interesting that our world focuses mostly on relationships. In the entertainment world, many movies, some good and some bad, focus on love stories. In the music industry, entertainers sell millions of records, with powerful lyrics singing about love, love, love. I'm reminded of the song "I Have to Respect the Power of Love." This R&B hit was first recorded by Stephanie Mills. Because of this song, I decided to name this message, The Power of Love.

Love permeates throughout the world as a force which needs, in some circumstances, to be reckoned with because of the world's sometimes misleading philosophy which begins and ends with physical attraction. Yet love is more than a physical attraction. The Bible says:

> Love suffers long and is kind; love does not envy; love does not parade itself, is not puffed up; does not behave rudely, does not seek its own, is not provoked, thinks no evil; does not rejoice in iniquity, but rejoices in the truth; bears all things, believes all things, hopes all things, endures all things. Love never fails (1Corinthians 13:4-8).

The Bible says, "Love never fails" (1Corninthians 13:8). This love is from the love of God. This is a different type of love. This is *agape* love. *Agape* is one of several Greek words meaning love. Love your neighbor as yourself. This does not mean that love, romantic love, between two people doesn't exist. But, it is classified as something else. I do not want to minimize its purpose or its power. Yet, the love which Jesus speaks of, teaches us to love our neighbors as well as our enemies. That sometimes can be a big pill to swallow.

In the book of Matthew, Jesus said:

> You have heard that it was said, "You shall love your neighbor and hate your enemy." But I say to you, love your enemies, bless those who curse you, do good to those who hate you, and pray for those who spitefully use you and persecute you, that you may be sons of your Father in heaven; for He makes His sun rise on the evil and on the good, and sends rain on the just and on the unjust. For if you love those who love you, what reward have you? Do not even the tax collectors do the same? And if you greet your brethren only, what do you do more than others? Do

not even the tax collectors do so? Therefore you shall be perfect, just as your Father in heaven is perfect (Matthew 5:43-48).

These passages are from the Sermon on the Mount. They reflect the true meaning of *agape* love.

I'm reminded of the Power of Love when Jesus died on the cross and arose on the third day. If you remember correctly, Jesus said, "Therefore My Father loves Me, because I lay down My life that I may take it again. No one takes it from Me, but I lay it down of Myself. I have power to lay it down, and I have power to take it again. This command I have received from My Father" (John 10:17-18). When you begin to understand the power that Jesus has, then you can say I Have Learned to Respect the Power of Love. There is no one in the history of the world who has the power that Jesus has on earth and in heaven. If you have faith to believe in the mystery – Christ died, Christ rose from the dead, and Christ will return for His bride, the church – then you can receive the gift of salvation. This is the best free gift in the world! Salvation gives you eternal life. You receive the Holy Spirit when you receive the gift of salvation and then you can qualify to receive the Baptism of the Holy Spirit with the evidence of speaking in tongues.

Love should be the essence of your being. It is significant in every aspect of life. As Christians, we should walk in love and obedience to Christ's commandments. When the lawyer challenged Jesus in Matthew 22, asking Jesus which is the greatest commandment he identifies his reluctance to obey Jesus' teaching.

The word of God says:

> But when the Pharisees heard that He had silenced the Sadducees, they gathered together. Then one of them, a lawyer asked Him a question, testing Him, and saying, "Teacher, which is the great commandment in the law?" Jesus said to him, "You shall love the Lord your God with all your heart, with all your soul, and with all your mind.' This is the first and great commandment. And the second is like it; 'You shall love your neighbor as yourself.' On these two commandments hangs all the Law and the Prophets" (Matthew 22:34-40).

Your relationship with Jesus Christ should take priority in your life! Not your job, not your spouse, not your children, not your friends. You need to learn to Respect the Power of Love because Jesus laid down His life for you and there is no greater love than the love of God. You must rely on Him. You must trust Him. You must acknowledge Him. You must love Him because He first loved you.

Many times people make excuses about why they can't come to Christ right now. They want to get right, then come to Jesus. But it is only through Christ that we can reach a place of sanctification, purification and holiness. It is only through Him that we can receive eternal life. It is only through Him, that we can love Him with all of our heart, soul and mind and love our neighbors as ourselves. It is only through Him that we can fulfill His plan for our lives.

A Few Minutes With God

Jesus said:

> This is My commandment, that you love one another as I have loved you. Greater love has no one than this, than to lay down one's life for his friends. You are My friends if you do whatever I command you. No longer do I call you servants, for a servant does not know what his master is doing; but I have called you friends, for all things that I heard from My Father I have made known to you. You did not choose Me, but I chose you and appointed you that you should go and bear fruit, and that your fruit should remain, that whatever you ask the Father in My name He may give you. These things I command you, that you love one another (John 15:12-17).

Jesus is the only living Savior of the world. I invite you to receive Him today as your Personal Savior. Remember Valentine's Day will not only be just another day of giving but a day of receiving. You can receive the gift of salvation and eternal life. Sometimes your lives may make a U-turn because the Lord has a special assignment just for you. With such great love being spread on Valentine's Day, remember to spread the love of Jesus. Remember the cross. Remember Calvary. If you believe and receive the Lord Jesus, you will be able to say I Learn to Respect the Power of Love. Have a great day on Valentine's Day and remember to spread the love of Jesus Christ, the true Power of Love.

A Walk of Love, A Walk of Grace, A Walk of Faith

Ephesians 2:8-10/ Ephesians 2:8

"For by grace you have been saved through faith, and that not of yourselves; it is the gift of God."
(Ephesians 2:8 NKJV)

1. A WALK OF LOVE

The thirteenth chapter of the book of Corinthians talks about the importance of love. If I were to designate one verse that is most significant it would be verse 8: "Love never fails" (1Corinthians 13:8). Love was actually the focal point of Christ's death and resurrection. After the fall of man in the Garden of Eden, God sent His Son so that you may be redeemed from the curse of the law. Jesus is love in action.

John 3:16-17 declares "For God so loved the world that He gave His only begotten Son, that whoever believes in Him should not perish but have everlasting life. For God did not send His Son into the world to condemn the world, but that the world through Him might be saved."

If you choose to live a life without love, then you choose to live a life without God because God is love. All of you are in relationships. They may be parents and children, brothers and sisters, husbands and wives, boyfriends and girlfriends. You may have relationships with other family members including cousins, aunts, uncles, and in-laws. You may have friends from school, or friends from work, or friends from church or other associates or organizations that you belong to. It is very hard to live in a world, if you do not have any type of relationships with others.

Once you discover the power of love and the existence of love. You will find it to be a powerful source. When you connect to God as your source of power, then you are in the love zone. What is the love zone? It is your ability to connect with people through love. Jesus Christ connects with us through love. And yet many people misunderstand His purpose for dying on the cross. When Christ died on the cross He paid the ultimate sacrifice for us through love. It was a walk of love. It was a walk of faith. It was a walk of grace. When Jesus said: "I will never leave you nor forsake you" (Hebrews 13:5). This was a walk of love. When Jesus said: "You shall love your neighbor as yourself" (Matthew 22:39). This exhibited the love of Christ. If you understand the power and the significance of love, if you can grasp just a portion of the essence of love, then you can see the bond between yourself and your relationship with Christ. The Bible says, "But seek first the kingdom of God and His righteousness, and all these things shall be added to you" (Matthew 6:33).

I'm reminded of the words of James 1:26-27, "If anyone among you thinks he is religious, and does not bridle his tongue but deceives his own heart, this one's religion is useless. Pure and undefiled religion before God and the Father is this: to visit orphans and widows in their trouble, and to keep oneself unspotted from the world." Although this scripture does not mention the word love, to visit orphans and widows in their trouble and to keep oneself unspotted from the world is love in action.

2. A WALK OF GRACE

In Ephesians 2:8-10, Paul empowers us with these words: "For by grace you have been saved through faith, and that not of yourselves; it is the gift of God, not of works, lest anyone should boast. For we are His workmanship, created in Christ Jesus for good works, which God prepared beforehand that we should walk in them."

The walk of grace includes the walk of faith because the Bible says, "For by grace you have been saved through faith, and that not of yourselves; it is the gift of God, not of works, lest anyone should boast" (Ephesians 2:8-9). What is grace? It is simply unmerited favor. Grace means to be given something without works. Many speak of God's grace. It is the grace of God that allows you to be saved. It is the grace of God that saves you when you repent and when you ask Jesus to come into your heart.

To paraphrase the words of Paul in 2Corinthians 12:7-10, He said that he had a thorn in his flesh. He said that Satan buffeted him, or to understand the language – Satan was harassing him. Paul decided to go to Jesus about Satan three times. Then he said, to him, "My grace is sufficient for you for My strength is made perfect in weakness" (2Corinthians 12:9). Later in the passage Paul simply says, "For when I am weak, then I am strong" (2Corinthians 12:10).

The grace of God is sovereign. It is His sole purpose to provide grace, unmerited favor to His children. Grace is for the believer. Salvation is the gift to the believer. Grace is the vehicle that God uses to redeem the believer. John speaks of the laws of Moses in reference to the Ten Commandments. The Bible records these words. "For the law was given through Moses, but grace and truth came through Jesus Christ" (John 1:17). Remember A Walk Of Grace.

3. A WALK OF FAITH

In Romans 10:17 Apostle Paul says, "So then faith comes by hearing, and hearing by the word of God." This is an old familiar verse that is often quoted. Once you are born again, it is necessary to renew your mind in the word of God. Faith comes by hearing and hearing and *hearing* the word of God. There are many people who are spiritual babes because they do not take the time to study the word for themselves. I believe that it is the investigation of the word, the thirst for the word and the hunger for the word that will keep you anchored in the word. If you align yourself with the word of God, then you will discover the will of God for your life. Have you ever heard the saying "Money doesn't grow on trees"? That's a true statement. But if you don't know anything about trees, you may think that money grows on trees. This is really hypothetical, but the truth of the matter is that if you know that a tree is a plant that grows fruit then you can look for that specific type of fruit that the tree bears.

If you depend on everyone else to feed your spirit, you could starve spiritually. You may not know that your spirit can also bear fruit. The fruit of the spirit is mentioned in Galatians. Every day we are constantly bombarded with the news, both local and national. It has become a part of our daily culture.. We are bombarded with negative imagines, con artist, thieves, murderers, bad weather reports and ongoing wars.

    I want to remind you of the Good News of Jesus Christ. Let Him anchor the news in the afternoon before you look at the evening news. Why don't you fill your mind with the word of God? You can listen to a Christian CD or watch a DVD. You can read a Christian book or magazine. Or you can study the bible. Why? Because faith comes by hearing the word of God. If you know the word of God, then you can apply it to your daily life. If you know that Jesus Christ lives, then you will better understand His character and understand His will for your life.

I challenge you today to remember these 3 points:

    A WALK OF LOVE
    A WALK OF GRACE
    A WALK OF FAITH

These three steps will enhance your relationship with Jesus Christ.

Who's Knocking at Your Door?

Revelation 3:19-20/ Revelation 3:20

"Behold, I stand at the door, and knock: if any man hear my voice, and open the door, I will come in to him, and will sup with him, and he with me." (Revelation 3:20 KJV)

While growing up in our home, my parents taught my sister and me not to open the door unless we knew the person who stood on the other side. In other words, don't open the door to strangers. There are two questions I want to ask to you. The first one is: who's knocking at your door? Is it your neighbor? Is it your friend? Is it a thief? Or is it UPS with a special package? Or is it your long lost son, the prodigal son? I ask the question again my friends: who's knocking at your door?

The second question I want to ask is: how will you respond to the person at the door? If it is your neighbor, will you remember the verse in Leviticus 19:18, which states, "Thou shalt not avenge, not bear any grudge against the children of thy people, but thou shalt love thy neighbor as thyself: I am the Lord."

How would you respond to your friend? Will you remember Proverbs 18:24? "A man that hath friends must shew himself friendly: and there is a friend that sticketh closer than a brother." Jesus said in John 15:12-15

This is my commandment. That ye love one another, as I have loved you. Greater love hath no man than this, that a man lay down his life for his friends. Ye are my friends, if ye do whatsoever I command you. Henceforth I call you not servant; for the servant knoweth not what his lord doeth: but I have called you friends; for all things that I have heard of my Father I have made known unto you."

How will you respond to a thief? Jesus said in John 10:10, "The thief cometh not, but for to steal, and to kill, and to destroy: I am come that they might have life, and that they might have it more abundantly."

Who's knocking at your door today? Is it your long lost son? Someone who needed prayer and you have been interceding for him for many years and you discover he has become a changed man returning home with a new attitude. He is truly the prodigal son.

Who's knocking at your door? Jesus says, "Behold, I stand at the door, and knock: if any man hear my voice, and open the door, I will come in to him, and will sup with him, and he with me" (Revelation 3:20).

Who's knocking at your door? Often telemarketers will have the following ways in which someone will respond to their calls. There are several ways in which you can respond to them. There are several ways in which you can respond to Jesus. For example, I think to myself my name is Arlena D. Lee. I am calling on behalf of the Good News Inc. I'm calling to offer you the opportunity to hear the good news of the gospel of Jesus Christ. These are some of the ways that people will respond to Jesus when he knocks on their door. The first response is: not available. They will say that they are not available to talk. Some people's telephone lines will be busy. Some people will ask Jesus to call another day. And some people will let it go to voicemail.

How will you respond to Jesus knocking at your door? Sometimes Jesus will receive a courtesy call. The people respond by saying "do not call again," "wrong number," and just "not interested." And finally there are those who will say "Yes. I want to hear the good news of the gospel of Jesus Christ."

Jesus said, "my sheep hear my voice" (John 10:27). He said, "All that ever came before me are thieves and robbers: but the sheep did not hear them. I am the door: by me if any man enter in, he shall be saved, and shall go in and out, and find pasture" (John 10:8-9).

What are you waiting for? Having a personal relationship with Jesus Christ should be the most important thing in your life. God has big plans for you and yet you neglect to open the door of your heart as if Jesus was a stranger. Jesus is at your door right now. Why don't you open the door? He is waiting patiently for you. He is a gentleman. He will not break the door down. You must invite Him into your heart.

There's an old Negro spiritual called "Somebody's Knocking At Your Door." The song says:

Knocks like Jesus. Somebody's knocking at your door.

Can you hear him? Somebody's knocking at your door.

Answer Jesus. Somebody's knocking at your door.
Oh-oh sinner, why don't you answer?
Somebody's knocking at your door."

All of us will die one day. It is important that we prepare for death because as the old folks say, "That is a debt that we all must pay." If we choose not to let Jesus into our lives, then we choose death over life. Paul says, "For the wages of sin is death; but the gift of God is eternal life through Jesus Christ our Lord" (Romans 6:23). The Bible also says in John 3:36, "He that believeth in the Son hath everlasting life: and he that believeth not the Son shall not see life; but the wrath of God abideth on him."

Why not test Jesus? Try Jesus? I know he is the answer to all your needs. Jesus died for our sins and there is no question in my mind that he arose on the third day. The Apostle Creed says he ascended into heaven and sits on the right hand of God the father almighty. He is Alpha and Omega. He is the beginning and the end. He is the Messiah. He's hope for the hopeless. He's bread to the hungry. He's a father to the fatherless. He's Jehoviah Jirah, my provider. He's waiting for you to open the door. He's knocking on the door of your heart right now.

Why don't you let him into your life? He is not a stranger, but he is the Lamb of God who takes away the sins of the world. Why walk in darkness when you could walk with Jesus who is the light of the world. Jesus is knocking at your door right now.

A Few Minutes With God

Isaiah 53:3 reads, "He is despised and rejected of men; a man of sorrows, and acquainted with grief: and we hid as it were our faces from him; he was despised, and we esteemed him not." Isaiah 53:7 reminds us that Jesus was "Oppressed, and He was afflicted, Yet He opened not His mouth: He is brought as a lamb to the slaughter, and as a sheep before her shearers is dumb, so he openeth not his mouth." If you understand the price Jesus paid on the cross, you would know the value of having a personal relationship with Jesus Christ. He is the answer. He is the way, the truth and the life. This was God's Son, the same Son who can set you free, the same Son who is knocking on your door.

Do you remember Sojourner Truth who heard the voice of Jesus? She was an abolitionist and agitator for women's rights. Do you remember Harriet Tubman who heard the voice of Jesus as she guided more than 300 slaves to freedom through the Underground Railroad? Do you remember Mary McLeod Bethune, who heard the voice of Jesus when she founded my alma mater in 1904 with five little girls, a dollar and a half, and faith in God? Her legacy lives on at Bethune Cookman University.

Do you remember Martin Luther King, who heard the voice of Jesus when he stood at the Lincoln Memorial and said, "I have a dream"? The last words of that speech are:

> ...when we allow freedom ring, when we let it ring from every village and every hamlet, from every state and every city, we will be able to speed up that day when all of God's children, black men and white men, Jews and Gentiles, Protestants and Catholics, will be

able to join hands and sing in the words of the old Negro spiritual:

Free at last! Free at last!
Thank God Almighty, we are free at last!

Why can't you hear the voice of Jesus today? He is knocking at your door. He is knocking at the door of your hearts. The question I want to ask you today is: when will you open the door?

There's A Gift In Your Womb

Jeremiah 1:1-19/Jeremiah 1:5

"Before I formed you in the womb I knew you; Before you were born I sanctified you; I ordained you a prophet to the nations."
(Jeremiah 1:5 NKJV)

On Mother's Day, I want to say to each of you who are mothers and grandmothers and stepmothers – Happy Mother's Day! I want to acknowledge all of you who have taken the responsibility of raising a child. It is one of the greatest responsibilities in life. I want to acknowledge my own mother who is a positive influence in my life. I want to speak to mothers today on a personal level and on a prophetic level.

Now mothers, what was your first reaction when the doctor told you that you were going to have a baby? Think back. Did you laugh? Did you cry? Did you shout? Or did you say, "It couldn't be?" Did you say to the doctor just like Hattie McDaniel's character in *Gone with the Wind*, "I don't know nothing 'bout birthin' no babies!" Some of you might have to think way back. Some of you may remember the day and the time immediately and vividly. I just want you to think back to that day and remember your reactions. On that day, you may not have received this revelation but, on that day, you found out that there was a gift in your womb. The gift of life was implanted in your womb by God, the creator of life.

A Few Minutes With God

Hear the words of Jeremiah, "Then the word of the Lord came to me, saying: Before I formed you in the womb I knew you; Before you were born I sanctified you; I ordained you a prophet to the nations" (Jeremiah 1:4-5 NKJV). The person who emerged from your womb is your son or daughter. Birthed from the protection of your womb into the world. Although, I have no children; I want to offer this advice. If your children are not yet adults, allow your child to experience life, talk to them and communicate with them. Allow them to tell you how they feel. If we, meaning the family lack nothing else, it is the lack of communication with parents. Be open, be honest, and challenge your children. They are a gift from God. If God knew your child before he formed him in your womb, then he knows his strengths and weaknesses. He knows his abilities and disabilities. He knows even his thoughts, his fears, and his anxieties. I believe the Lord has brought this to my attention because of the staggering statistics that are quoted as scripture through the media.

According to CNN, six thousand children drop out of school every day, about 1 million per year. Is the African American child forever lost? Or is he simply crying out for help and in need of a new direction? You can be his or her trainer. There should not be a dilemma about what time to go to bed, what time to do homework, or what time to turn off the TV. There should be rules about what to watch on TV and what movies to go to. There should be a time to turn off the computer. There should be time set aside to read books and magazines, and even to have a devotional time reading the Bible. There should be time to have a social life.

Why is the African American child struggling? Is it too late? What's going on in your home? Proverbs 22:6 NKJV says, "Train up a child in the way he should go, And when he is old he will not depart from it." Training takes time and perseverance and patience on the part of the parents.

Allow your child to discover his own gifts and talents, and encourage them. Just because you work in a certain profession does not mean your child will, or must, take an interest in it. Expose him to different types of opportunities. I mentioned the prophet Jeremiah, and you may say, "Hey Rev. Lee, How does this scripture relate to me? My child is not a prophet." Before your child was born, God ordained him for a purpose. It is your job to train him in the ways of the Lord. Teach him and talk to him about your relationship with Jesus Christ and encourage him to go to church, Sunday school and Bible Study. As a minister, I want to be able to analyze, investigate, and teach the Word with simplicity and authority so that even children will come to Jesus Christ. Teach your child to trust God and to depend on God. Teach your child to communicate with God through prayer.

The first chapter Luke describes the birth of John the Baptist. When Elizabeth his mother gave birth to him, her neighbors and cousins rejoiced with her. On the eighth day, they circumcised John and wanted to name him Zacharias, after his father. However, Elizabeth said that no the child shall be named John which was a part of the custom during that time. But, the relatives and friends said that no one in the family was named John. So they made signs to his father, Zacharias who had been mute since the Angel Gabriel appeared to him. The Angel Gabriel told him before the birth of John, although Elizabeth was barren, she would bear a child even though she was well advanced in age and she would have a son and his name would be John. The Angel Gabriel told him that his son would be filled with the Holy Spirit from his mother's womb and that this child John would turn many of the children of Israel to the Lord, going before Jesus in the spirit and power of Elijah, to turn the fathers to the children, and the disobedient to the wisdom of the Just, to make ready a people prepared for the Lord.

Zacharias did not believe Gabriel because he was an old man and his wife was an old woman. Gabriel told him that he was sent by God, but now because of his unbelief, he would be mute and be unable to speak until these events occurred.

This is why Zacharias was mute when John the Baptist was born. To paraphrase: He asked for a tablet to write on and he wrote "his name is John" and immediately his mouth was opened and he spoke and praised God. Then fear came over all of Judea. People were astonished saying what manner of child is this? And the Lord was with them. Then Zacharias was filled with the Holy Spirit and began to prophesy about his son, John the Baptist, who would prepare the people for the coming of the Lord.

All of you know about the story of the birth of Jesus. This story is told every year at Christmas. His birth was supernatural because he was born of the Virgin Mary. The angel Gabriel was sent by God to Mary to announce to her that she was highly favored and blessed among women, and she would conceive in her womb and bring forth a Son, and he would be called Jesus. She was puzzled by this and asked Gabriel the question, "How can this be, since I do not know a man?" And the angel answered and said to her "The Holy Spirit will come upon you, and the power of the Highest will overshadow you; therefore, also, that Holy One who is to be born will be called the Son of God" (Luke 1:34-35 NKJV).

A Few Minutes With God

What about the womb experience? Motherhood, I believe is not accidental. Inside your womb is placed the gift of life. It is your job to love, nurture and train your children. It is also your job to help them to reinforce the positive, to encourage them to discover themselves, to help them to dream the impossible dream. Life in the womb creates a supernatural bond. Only God can create your child. Only God can save your child. Teach him to put God first. Teach him to lean and depend on God, and to trust God. It is only the creator who can fix it if he's in trouble. Teach him to ask for wisdom, to study the bible, to ask God for guidance, protection and favor.

Most children don't spend more than 9 months in the womb. If you train your child in the ways of the Lord, he will not depart from it. Thank God for each of you who have birthed a child, because inside of you may be the next entrepreneur, the next principal, the next governor, the next lawyer, the next teacher, the next minister, the next talk show host, or even the next president of the United States of America. God has called your child for a specific purpose and he has a specific plan for his life. Therefore God will place a specific anointing on his life according to his gifts and talents to perform his earthly assignment.

"Then the word of the Lord came to me saying: Before I formed you in the womb I knew you; Before you were born I sanctified you; I ordained you a prophet to the nations" (Jeremiah 1:4-5 NKJV). And this is my prophecy to you. It is not profound but, it is certain that if you teach your child about Jesus Christ and he receives Jesus Christ as his Personal Savior, he becomes a part of another family: the Body of Christ. If you teach your child to serve the Lord and acknowledge Him in everything he does, I will guarantee that his life will never be the same as he learns to hear the voice of God and go where God says go and do what God says do. Your child will have an extraordinary life serving God. Thank God for the mother who has the gift of life in her womb. And thank God for Jesus Christ who gives us eternal life and the Holy Spirit who will guide you in everything that you do in life.

Guess Who's Coming to Dinner?

Luke 22:7-14/Luke 22:14-15

When the hour had come, He sat down, and the twelve apostles with Him. Then He said to them, "With fervent desire I have desired to eat this Passover with you before I suffer"
(Luke 22:14-15 NKJV)

Guess Who's Coming to Dinner is a poignant tale of an interracial relationship. It premiered in theaters in December 1967 and it stars Sidney Poitier, Katherine Hepburn, and Spencer Tracy. Interestingly, and ironically enough, it played in the movies one year before Dr. Martin Luther King Jr. would be assassinated.

As the story unfolds, portraying a situation or circumstance which was unusual during the late sixties. Imagine your daughter flying home with the intentions of marrying someone of another race. Sydney Poitier plays the debonair doctor who met a woman on a trip in Hawaii and after 10 days decides to accompany her to her home to meet her parents, who are be played by Spencer Tracy and Katherine Hepburn. Poitier's character's intention was to get their approval for marriage.

After meeting the family, the mother agreed to support her daughter but the father had difficulty agreeing to the situation. In the midst of it all, the doctor spoke to his parents over the phone and his new fiancé encouraged him to invite them to dinner. Later, as they arrived at the airport, they were quickly introduced to the situation when their son introduced them to his fiancé who was Caucasian or to make it plain: she was white.

Once they reached the home of her parents, there were several times when both parents had conversations with each other, as well as their son and daughter. The father, played by Spencer Tracy, had invited his friend the Monsignor to come to dinner after canceling their regular weekend golf game. The end of the movie finds them all sitting down at the dinner table.

Some of you may remember this popular film; it won an Academy Award. Now you may ask the question: what does this movie have to do with our Lord and Savior Jesus Christ?

In the book of Luke, Jesus and his disciples were preparing for the Passover. The Bible says:

> Then came the Day of Unleavened Bread, when the Passover must be killed. And He sent Peter and John, saying, "Go and prepare the Passover for us, that we may eat." So they said to Him, "Where do You want us to prepare?" And He said to them, "Behold, when you have entered the city, a man will meet you carrying a pitcher of water; follow him into the house which he enters. Then you shall say to the master of the house, 'The teacher says to you, "Where is the guest room where I may eat the Passover with My disciples?"' Then he will show you a large, furnished upper room; there make ready." So they went and

found it just as He had said to them, and they prepared the Passover (Luke 22:7-13 NKJV).

The Passover was in fact the last time Jesus would gather with His disciples before the crucifixion. In essence, the disciples were preparing for The Last Supper. The divine plan of God was executed in the upper room. All of His disciples assembled in the room. The names of the twelve disciples you will find in Matthew 10:2-4 NKJV:

> Now the names of the twelve apostles are these: first, Simon, who is called Peter, and Andrew his brother; James the son of Zebedee, and John his brother; Philip and Bartholomew; Thomas and Matthew the tax collector; James the son of Alphaeus, and Lebbaeus, whose surname was Thaddaeus; Simon the Cananite, and Judas Iscariot, who betrayed Him.

Guess who's coming to dinner? All of the disciples were there in the upper room to eat The Last Supper with Jesus before he would lay down His life for all mankind.

The book of Exodus reveals the significance of the Passover. God passed over the house of the Israelites during the Final Plague of the Ten Plagues of Egypt. The Bible states that on the night of the Plagues, the Israelites smeared their lintels and doorposts with the blood of the Passover sacrifice which is usually a lamb or a kid. Only those who were first born who had the blood on the doorpost were spared or passed over. The Jewish Tradition still recognizes and celebrates the Passover. Furthermore, in Luke 22:14-23 NKJV, the Bible says:

When the hour had come, He sat down, and the twelve apostles with Him. Then He said to them, "With fervent desire I have desired to eat this Passover with you before I suffer. For I say to you, I will no longer eat of it until it is fulfilled in the kingdom of God." Then He took the cup, and gave thanks, and said, "Take this and divide it among yourselves; for I say to you, I will not drink of the fruit of the vine until the kingdom of God comes." And He took bread, gave thanks and broke it, and gave it to them, saying, "This is My body which is given for you; do this in remembrance of Me." Likewise He also took the cup after supper, saying, "This cup is the new covenant in My blood, which is shed for you. But behold, the hand of My betrayer is with Me on the table. And truly the Son of Man goes as it has determined, but woe to that man by whom He is betrayed!" Then they began to question among themselves, which of them it was who would do this thing.

I remember as a child, our family would always eat dinner together. It was a very significant time to discuss the events of the day. It played a major part in my life knowing that I could express my opinions and receive kudos even from my own family. Now, I am in the Body of Christ and if you are in the Body of Christ, we are able to come to the communion table. A common practice is to have communion or The Last Supper on the first Sunday of each month. The Bible states in 1Corinthians 11:28-29 NKJV, "But let a man examine himself, and so let him eat of the bread and drink of the cup. For he who eats and drinks in an unworthy manner eats and drinks judgment to himself, not discerning the Lord's body." We must understand the symbolic significance of eating and drinking the body and blood of Christ remembering that He is the Lamb of God who takes away the sins of the world.

Guess Who's Coming to Dinner? Well, it probably won't be Sydney Poitier! But, if you are a born again Christian, I am inviting you to the Lord's Table, for the Last Supper, where Jesus said, "Do this in remembrance of me" (1Corinthians 11:24).

Have You Caught Any Fish lately?

Matthew 4:18-21/ Matthew 4:19

Then He said to them, "Follow Me, and I will make you fishers of men." (Matthew 4:19 NKJV)

One of my favorite foods in the world is fish. I developed a love of fish as a child. We would have fried fish, that southern dish every Friday night. Fish and grits and a few hush puppies seasoned to taste. My father's family was born on an island called Red Fish Point in Panama City, Florida, and they were commercial fishermen. They ate fish day and night. I remember going to the family reunions where I would beg my mother for a hamburger. Because we had only one choice of meat at the picnic, one choice of meat at the banquet, and only one choice of meat when we were visiting friends and relatives. That choice, of course, was fish.

I must admit that as the years passed by I began to acquire a taste for red snapper and grouper and trout and catfish, but I shied away from the backbones, preferring that tail end which does not have many bones. Even now on the weekends, you will see various organizations selling fish sandwiches throughout the community and during special events. Selling fish sandwiches still remains a good way to make some quick cash as long as you have the hot sauce and mustard to go with it!

A Few Minutes With God

One of my father's favorite hobbies was to go fishing. He would rise early in the morning, call his fishing buddies and they would spend the day fishing. Sometimes they would go in the boat, or sometimes they would wade in the water other times they would just go to the pier and throw their rods over the rail. Sometimes Dad would come home empty handed and sometimes we would eat fish for days. The interesting thing about fishing is that you have to have the right kind of bait to catch the fish. The purpose of the bait is to lure the fish to the bait so that you can hook the fish, therefore realizing a great supper.

Now, let's turn our attention to the word of God. Matthew describes how Jesus recruited His disciples. Jesus recruited Simon and his brother Andrew telling them, "Follow Me, and I will make you fishers of men" (Matthew 4:19). They left their nets and followed Jesus. In the same way, Jesus recruited James the Son of Zebedee, and John his brother who left the boat and their father and followed Jesus. So many times we hear about people who have a call or know in their spirit that God has called them to do something special in life. Yet many resist refuse, ignore, or run away from God's will in their life. Matthew chooses to mention only four of the twelve disciples, but they left their jobs and their families immediately and followed Jesus.

This was not the case with the Prophet Jonah. When God told Jonah to go to Nineveh he did not want to go. So he disobeyed the Lord and went to Joppa, boarded a ship, and headed for Tarshish. He ended up being thrown overboard and swallowed by a fish. He stayed in the fish for three days and three nights. After Jonah prayed, the Lord told the fish to spit Jonah out on dry land. Jonah heard the voice of the Lord again to go to Nineveh. This time he obeyed and went to preach in Nineveh completing his assignment. Jonah's task was to preach to the wicked city of Nineveh. After he preached, the people believed and put on sackcloths and fasted. The king of Nineveh took off his robe and put on sackcloths and sat in ashes. The king declared that no one should eat or drink, but cry out to God and let everyone turn from evil. They were hoping that God would not continue to be angry so that they would not perish. God changed his mind after he saw their good works, and did not bring the disaster that he had planned.

Jonah was unhappy with God's decision, so he prayed to God, reminding him that he fled to Tarshish knowing that he was a God who was slow to anger and abundant in love. Therefore, Jonah asked the Lord to take his life from him, wishing to die. The Lord asked Jonah "Is it right for you to be angry?" (Jonah 4:4) Jonah went out of the city and sat down. The Lord provided a plant to shade him. Then the next morning the Lord placed a worm on the plant so that it withered away. After the plant was damaged, the sun arose, and there was a violent east wind causing Jonah to feel faint. He then again wished to die rather than live:

> Then God said to Jonah, "Is it right for you to be angry about the plant?" And he said, "It is right for me to be angry, even to death!" But the Lord said, "You have had pity on the plant for which you have not labored, nor made it grow, which came up in a night and perished in a night. "And should I not pity Nineveh, that great city, in which are more than one hundred and twenty thousand persons who cannot discern between their right hand and their left—and much livestock?" (Jonah 4:9-11 NKJV).

A Few Minutes With God

In the Lord's eyes, Jonah's anger was misconstrued because he had pity for a plant rather than for the people of Nineveh who turned from their wicked ways. This reaction caused the Lord to challenge Jonah's behavior. In other words, even though Jonah preached, he did not want God to have mercy on the people, so he agonized, turning his anger towards the Lord.

Well, what is the purpose of preaching? Is it not to spread God's word so that people will turn from their wicked ways? Jonah had several flaws yet God used him anyway. His first problem was that he heard the word of the Lord and fled, or ran the opposite way. The Bible doesn't say this, but Jonah was probably terrified after being thrown overboard and finding himself in the belly of a fish. After he was delivered and fulfilled his mission, he was still angry with God.

Sometimes the Lord calls the most unlikely person. Here in the Old Testament, you find Jonah the prophet refusing to obey until God took some drastic measures. Some of you may be like the disciples and some of you may be like Jonah. God works through your deepest emotions and regardless of fear, regardless of anger, regardless of frustrations or inadequacy, God can use you to be a witness to a friend, a neighbor, a family member, or even to a nation. Don't run from God. The Bible reads:

> Then Jesus said to His disciples, "If anyone desires to come after Me, let him deny himself, and take up his cross, and follow Me. For whoever desires to save his life will lose it, but whoever loses his life for My sake will find it. For what profit is it to a man if he gains the whole world, and loses his own soul? Or

what will a man give in exchange for his soul? For the Son of Man will come in the glory of His Father with His angels, and then He will reward each according to his works" (Matthew 16:24-27 NKJV).

Jonah was in danger of losing his life because of disobedience however God spared Jonah's life too. I chose the title of this message, "Have You Caught Any Fish Lately" to remind you that Jesus said to the disciples, "Follow Me, and I will make you fishers of men" (Matthew 4:19). John the Baptist, who paved the way for Jesus, declared that he came as a witness, to bear witness of the Light, that all would believe. His task was to provide a roadmap to Jesus Christ. It was just as if John the Baptist was a British subject blowing the trumpet to announce the coming of a king. John the Baptist announced the coming of Jesus Christ and to those Levites and priests who inquired about him. He said, "I am the voice of one crying in the wilderness: Make straight the way of the Lord" (John 1:23 NKJV).

We often hear people talk about purpose. What is your purpose in life? What is your gift or talent? What is your ambition? What is your passion? The disciples' passion was to provide an avenue for the souls of men to obtain eternal life. Whatever your gift or talent or ambition, if you are a child of God, I pray that you find it within your heart to tell somebody about Jesus. It is crucial that you realize that witnessing should be a part of the package. You might ask what package? Romans 10-9 NKJV says: "If you confess with your mouth the Lord Jesus and believe in your heart that God has raised Him from the dead, you will be saved. For with the heart one believes unto righteousness, and with the mouth confession is made unto salvation." Apostle Paul's instruction on salvation is exact.

Therefore, if you witness to people and show them the word of God, you may be able to catch some fish.

The Bible says, "The fruit of the righteous is a tree of life, And he who wins souls is wise" (Proverbs 11:30 NKJV). The good news is that you don't have to win souls by yourself. Jesus promises the Holy Spirit. He says, "But you shall receive power when the Holy Spirit has come upon you; and you shall be witnesses to Me in Jerusalem, and in all Judea and Samaria, and to the end of the earth" (Acts 1:8). So I am asking you today to take your bait, the Bible, and receive the power from the Holy Spirit. Now go out and catch some fish.

Tongues of Fire

Acts 2:1-4/ Acts 2:4

"And they were all filled with the Holy Ghost, and began to speak with other tongues, as the Spirit gave them utterance."
(Acts 2:4 KJV)

January of 2006 was a very special time for me. It is not only the celebration of Jesus' birthday and a New Year, but it is my 20th anniversary. No, not of marriage. That was the 20th year since I had been Baptized in the Holy Spirit with the evidence of speaking in tongues. I chose this subject purposefully, as well as hesitantly, because I realize that many churches are traditional denominational churches that do not teach about the gift of the Holy Spirit which the Bible says is available to everyone. Today, I can say that I come to you as a private investigator and a defense attorney on behalf of my Lord and Savior, Jesus Christ. I have investigated the scriptures and I am here on a divine assignment. I am asking you to go back to the Bible and study, ponder, and meditate on the scriptures that are clearly written in support of speaking in tongues in this new day. Today you must be the jury. Each individual that receives this word will be responsible to give a yea or nay after hearing the word of God today. I am cognizant of the fact that I have heard several negative sermons about speaking in tongues, and I also have observed scriptures which were not dealt with, but skipped over.

If in fact Jesus is the same yesterday, today and forever, then isn't it correct to believe that speaking in tongues is for today? It is not just a Pentecostal thing, strictly for that denomination is

Pentecostal. The Bible never suggests that the infilling of the Holy Ghost was only for them (meaning a specific group of people whose denomination is Pentecostal). In some circles, speaking in tongues is looked upon as an emotional, uncontrollable act, and since no one can necessarily interpret what is said, some people present it in a negative light. However, Paul states in 1Corinthians 14:2 KJV, "For he that speaketh in an unknown tongue speaketh not unto men, but unto God: for no man understandeth him; howbeit in the spirit he speaketh mysteries." 1Corinthians 14:4 says, "He that speaketh in an unknown tongue edifieth himself; but he that prophesieth edifieth the church."

Then why are tongues necessary? Why would God allow this teaching to be placed in the Bible or a part of the canon if it is not significant in today's world? You may ask what the purpose and benefits of speaking in tongues are. Paul says in 1Corinthians 14:13-15, "Wherefore let him that speaketh in an unknown tongue pray that he may interpret. For if I pray in an unknown tongue, my spirit prayeth, but my understanding is unfruitful. What is it then? I will pray with the spirit, and I will pray with the understanding also: I will sing with the spirit, and I will sing with the understanding also." The scriptures also say in 1Corinthians 14:28, "But if there be no interpreter, let him keep silent in the church; and let him speak to himself, and to God."

There are several benefits to speaking in tongues, according to several men of God who are noted in the Christian world. Kenneth E. Hagin, for example makes an interesting statement in his book, *The Baptism in the Holy Spirit*. He writes:

The word of God teaches that when we are filled with the Holy Spirit we speak with other tongues as the Spirit gives utterance. Tongues is an initial evidence or sign of the Baptism in the Holy Spirit. Therefore, the first reason people should speak with other tongues is because this is a supernatural evidence of the Spirit's indwelling (page 41).

Therefore, you will experience the infilling as God's supernatural gift to you. When you pray in tongues, you pray the perfect will of God. In Romans 8:26, Paul addresses this issue by saying, "Likewise the Spirit also helpeth our infirmities: for we know not what we should pray for as we ought: but the Spirit itself maketh intercession for us with groanings which cannot be uttered." When you pray in tongues you are not praying with articulate speech. The Holy Ghost makes intercession for us in groanings. In other words you are speaking directly to God.

Let's look at another example in the Acts of the Apostles.

Acts 2:38-39 reads, "Then Peter said unto them, Repent, and be baptized every one of you in the name of Jesus Christ for the remission of sins, and ye shall receive the gift of the Holy Ghost. For the promise is unto you, and to your children, and to all that are afar off, even as many as the Lord our God shall call." Let us understand the significance of this scripture. Before you can receive the gift of the Holy Ghost you must be born again. That is the only prerequisite for receiving the gift of the Holy Spirit. Notice closely that the Bible says you must receive the gift which has already been given at Pentecost. First you are saved. Then you are filled. There are a number of names that you might see or hear which relate to the

Baptism in the Holy Spirit such as being spirit-filled, receiving the Holy Spirit, the baptism in the Holy Spirit, or being filled with the Holy Spirit. All of these names refer to the gift of the Holy Spirit.

In many traditional churches, we are taught that when you are born again you have the Holy Ghost and there is no separate infilling subsequent to salvation. However, I beg to differ because I received the Baptism of the Holy Spirit with the evidence of speaking in tongues while I was a Baptist. Therefore, I must conclude that it does not matter if you are a part of a certain denomination. Furthermore, evidence throughout the Bible and my own experience has taught me that you can be filled regardless of denomination, status in life, race, or background. The infilling of the Holy Ghost is available to you if you have first been born again. In actuality, you are the beneficiary of the gift of the Holy Spirit. Just as Jesus died and rose again for our sins, it is justifiable and available to you once you are born again. The Bible tells us in 1Corinthians 14:22, "Wherefore tongues are for a sign, not to them that believe, but to them that believe not: but prophesying serveth not for them that believe not, but for them which believe."

I want you to be aware of this revelation which, in fact, was brought to my attention several years ago as I was studying the Bible. If in fact you understand the Bible, it presents the trinity as we understand it as God the Father, Jesus his Son and The Holy Ghost who is a Spirit and the third person of the Godhead. Although the word trinity is not found in the Bible this word has been accepted by biblical scholars. Now, what is significant about the trinity is that each person of the Godhead presents itself, it is clear that there are certain places in the Bible where there is one dominate person. For example, Genesis 1:2 reads, "And the earth was without form, and void: and darkness was upon the face of the deep. And the Spirit of God moved upon the face of the waters." The first book of the Bible introduces God and The Holy Spirit. Yet Jesus is prophesied about in the Old Testament although he had not been born. Therefore, the prophet Isaiah says in Isaiah 7:14, "Therefore the Lord himself shall give you a sign; Behold a virgin shall conceive, and bear a son, and shall call his name Immanuel."

Jesus was prophesied about but did not come on the scene until the New Testament. He began his ministry at about age 30 and He is the dominate person in the New Testament for three years. He fulfilled his purpose by dying on the cross for our sins and he arose from the dead on the third day. Here is my point: when Jesus ascended into heaven, he promised the Holy Spirit. In John 14:15-18 NKJV, Jesus says:

> If you love Me, keep my commandments. And I will pray the Father, and he will give you another Helper (KJV uses the word "Comforter"), that He may abide with you forever- the Spirit of truth, whom the world cannot receive, because it neither sees Him nor knows Him but you know Him, for He dwells with you and will be in you. I will not leave you orphans: I will come to you.

To understand the revelation, you must understand a more intimate and personal relationship with God. We must not only receive the gift of salvation, but Jesus has provided a bonus gift: the Baptism of the Holy Spirit in which the initial evidence is speaking in tongues. It is from the drawing of the Holy Spirit that we receive the gift of salvation. In Ephesians 2:10 Paul says, "For by grace are ye saved through faith; and that not of yourselves: it is the gift of God." Salvation is the gift of God and the Baptism of the Holy Spirit is the gift of God. In each case we must choose to accept and receive these gifts.

When we are born again we are born of the Spirit of God. The experience that you can receive is subsequent, which means it comes after salvation and is the Baptism of the Holy Spirit. Let me make this clear: You do not have to speak in tongues to go to heaven, but this is a supernatural gift which provides a prayer language that is available to you because of Pentecost. There are several ways you may become spirit-filled. They include: laying on of hands, asking Jesus to fill you with the Holy Spirit, and receiving the gift. Paul states in 1Corinthians 14:5, "I would that ye all spake with tongues." Many people do not receive both gifts at the same time. Once someone is born again, there is usually a period of time before he receives the Baptism of the Holy Spirit with evidence of speaking in tongues.

Many times, we diminish the significance of speaking in tongues. It is either ignored or ostracized or people criticize those who speak in tongues because of personal ignorance or misunderstanding the word of God. Many believe that speaking in tongues is not for this modern day. Yet, there is evidence in the scriptures that gives examples of people in the Bible who spoke in tongues. Here's my argument: if in fact Jesus is the same, yesterday, today and forever and the word of God is relevant 2000 years after Jesus walked the face of the earth, why eliminate the power if it is available to receive? Realizing that this supernatural power gives you the power from within yourself to be a witness or preach the

Good News of the Gospel of Jesus Christ, why don't you thirst for it?

In Acts 1:8 Jesus said, "But ye shall receive power, after that the Holy Ghost is come upon you: and ye shall be witnesses unto me both in Jerusalem, and in all Judaea, and in Samaria, and unto the uttermost part of the earth."

Several Things to Remember about the Baptism of the Holy Spirit:

1. You must be born again.
2. You cannot receive the Baptism of the Holy Spirit unless you are born again.
3. The common initial evidence that you have received the Baptism of the Holy Spirit is that you speak in tongues.
4. Another name for speaking in tongues is called the prayer language.
5. You will not understand what you are saying when you speak in tongues because you are speaking directly to God and not to man.
6. The Baptism of the Holy Spirit is available to everyone regardless of denomination, race, or background. God is no respecter of person.
7. The Baptism of the Holy Spirit gives you the power to live victoriously, the power to serve, and the power to witness.

8. The Baptism of the Holy Spirit gives you the fullness of the Holy Spirit which gives you authority of power.

Remember the words in Acts 2:4, "And they were all filled with the Holy Ghost, and began to speak with other tongues, as the Spirit gave them utterance."

Circumstantial Evidence

John 9:1-12/ John 9:8

"Therefore the neighbors and those who previously had seen that he was blind said, is not this he who sat and begged?"
(John 9:8 NKJV)

I want to focus on Circumstantial Evidence. The story described in John 9:1-41 is about a man who was born blind, but Jesus healed him. Jesus "Spat on the ground and made clay with the saliva; and He anointed the eyes of the blind man with the clay. And He said to him, 'Go, wash in the pool of Siloam' (which is translated, Sent). So he went and washed and came back seeing." Then the Bible says, "Therefore the neighbors and those who previously had seen that he was blind said, 'Is not this he who sat and begged?' Some said, 'This is he.' Others said, 'He is like him.' He said, 'I am he'" (John 9:8-9).

People questioned the blind man as if it was an impossible act that he was born blind and now after he washed in the pool of Siloam he could see. The neighbors seemed perplexed as though they could not comprehend the fact that this man was blind and now he could see. This story I want to deem as circumstantial evidence.

First, the disciples asked Jesus when they saw the blind man, "Who sinned, this man or his parents, that he was born blind?" Jesus answered, "Neither this man nor his parents sinned, but that the works of God should be revealed in him. I must work the works of Him who sent Me while it is day; the night is coming when no one can work. As long as I am in the world, I am the light of the world" (John 9:2-5).

So let's analyze the situation for a moment. You know they have that news show called the *Situation Room*. So I want you to understand the situation. The bottom line is Jesus healed a man who was born blind and this healing miracle was being questioned by the status quo. In other words, the Pharisees who were the religious leaders questioned the blind man. The first problem was that Jesus healed the blind man on the Sabbath. The Pharisees questioned the legitimacy of the healing because it was done on the Sabbath. They said that this man, meaning Jesus, was not of God because He did not keep the Sabbath. The Sabbath was supposed to be a day of rest and there were certain things according to the Jewish Sabbath that you were not suppose to do. The irony of the matter is that the Pharisees thought the healing of the blind man was work rather than an act of love and compassion. Some of the other Pharisees said about Jesus, "How can a man who is a sinner do such signs? (John 9:16). So therefore the Pharisees were divided among themselves.

The Pharisees said to the blind man again, "What do you say about Him because He opened your eyes?" He said, "He is a prophet." But the Jews did not believe concerning him (John 9:17-18). So they spoke to the parents and asked them if the blind man was their son and if he was blind from birth. The parents said, "Yes this is our son and he was blind from birth." But then the Pharisees asked the question, "How does your son see now?" The parents of the blind man said that they did not know how their son received his sight and told the Jews to go ask him because he was of age to answer for himself.

In reality, his parents were afraid to answer the question because they did not want to be put out of the synagogue for confessing that Jesus was Christ. So the Pharisees, called the blind man again and said, "Give God the Glory! We know that this man is a sinner" (John 9:24). In the story in John 9:25-41, they were speaking of Jesus. The blind man said, "I don't know whether he is a sinner or not, but I was blind and now I see." They continuously asked the blind man, "What did Jesus do? How were your eyes opened?" It seems as though the blind man became agitated and said, "I already told you what happened and you did not listen." The blind man asked them did they want to become disciples and they said, "You are His disciple but we are Moses' disciples. We know that God spoke to Moses, as for this fellow, we do not know where He is from." The man answered and said to them, "Why, this is a marvelous thing, that you do not know where He is from; yet He has opened my eyes! Now we know that God does not hear sinners; but if anyone is a worshiper of God and does His will, He hears him." Since the world began it has been unheard of that anyone opened the eyes of one who was born blind. "If this Man were not from God, He could do nothing." They answered and said to him, "You were completely born in sins, and are you teaching us?" And they cast him out.

Jesus heard that they had cast him out; and when He had found him, He said to him, "Do you believe in the Son of God?" He answered and said, "Who is He, Lord, that I may believe in Him?" And Jesus said to him, "You have both seen Him and it is He who is talking with you." Then he said, "Lord I believe!" And he worshiped Him. And Jesus said, "For judgment I come into this world, that those who do not see may see, and that those who see may be made blind." Then some of the Pharisees who were with Him heard these words, and said to Him, "Are we blind also?" Jesus said to them, "If you were blind, you would have no sin; but now you say, 'We see.' Therefore your sins remains."

There are several issues that I would like to emphasize concerning this story, one being this healing miracle that John speaks about. It opens the door to the unenviable position of the Pharisees. In other words, the Pharisees rejected the idea or notion that Jesus actually performed this miracle and also had the audacity to do it on the Sabbath day. According to Jewish tradition this day should have been an exclusive day of rest. One thing that I noticed while reading and studying this lesson is that there were no eye witnesses that saw Jesus heal the blind man. This is why I coined the phrase or title of the message as Circumstantial Evidence which may take a theological twist from the point of the Pharisees. If we go back to the passage of scripture in John 9, it says that disciples questioned Jesus about the blind man. "Who sinned, this man or his parents?" (John 9:2). Although the disciples asked the question and Jesus answered them and then proceeded to heal the blind man, the Bible does not say whether the disciples were present at the scene. Some of the controversy with the Pharisees may also include (but not mentioned in the Bible) the fact that there were no eyewitnesses to the healing. Therefore, the healing could be deemed circumstantial. The definition of circumstantial evidence according to *dictionary.com* is "evidence not bearing directly on the fact in dispute, but various attendant circumstances from which the judge or jury might infer the occurrences of the fact in dispute." There was always controversy about Jesus and His acts of kindness and His authoritative posture. He challenged those who challenged Him because He knew that He was the Christ and He said, immediately "As long as I am in the world, I am the light of the world" (John

9:5). Jesus said, "I must work the works of Him who sent Me while it is day; the night is coming when no one can work" (John 9:4).

The Pharisees misconstrued the fact that Jesus has the power to heal. Jesus Christ came on earth to preach, teach, and to heal those who were sick as well as to perform miracles of nature. Matthew 4:23-24 says:

> And Jesus went about all Galilee, teaching in their synagogues, preaching the gospel of the kingdom, and healing all kinds of sickness and all kinds of disease among the people. Then His fame went throughout all Syria; and they brought to Him all sick people who were afflicted with various diseases and torments, and those who were demon-possessed, epileptics, and paralytics; and He healed them.

The Pharisees would not accept the fact that Jesus had actually performed a miracle and they did not believe that Jesus was God Himself in the flesh. Therefore, they refused to accept the healing as an act of God through Jesus Christ. Also, their reaction causes controversy among themselves as well as denying not only the healing, but also the authenticity and the authority of the healing power of Jesus Christ.

Even in the 21st century, there are folks who do not believe in the supernatural power of healing. There are specific scriptures in the Bible as well as multiple stories speaking to the issue of the healing power of Jesus. If you take those scriptures and apply them to your own life, to your own disease, then you can experience the supernatural healing power of Christ.

Another issue is that the blind man did not only receive a physical healing, but he was also enlightened because of his spiritual understanding. He believed that Jesus was a prophet and he was the Son of God. And this is how the Pharisees tried to challenge his beliefs as though he was ignorant. This remains to be an issue today because many people pick and choose the scriptures to believe and chop up the Bible like chop suey and then expect a miracle instead of embracing the scriptures as medicine to your body. I don't want to sound insensitive, but my point is if you have the faith to be saved by grace, you should also have the faith to be healed.

Often we have to be healed by traditional ways, by taking a series of test, receiving the diagnosis, and taking medicine or even having surgery. Is this supernatural healing also? I believe that Jesus can guide a surgeon's hand, that he can give your doctor wisdom to treat you with the proper medications. Therefore, to me, even a gradual healing is supernatural. It may not be instant, but it can be a permanent healing. Many do not neglect the wisdom of man. Therefore, don't neglect the healing power of Jesus Christ.

My last point is to acknowledge the blind man's testimony. This man stuck to his story that after Jesus "spat on the ground and made clay with the saliva; and He anointed the eyes of the blind man with the clay. And He said to him, 'Go, wash in the pool of Siloam' (which is translated Sent). So he went and washed, and came back seeing" (John 9:6-7). The evidence is that the blind man received his sight. He did not vary his testimony that Jesus opened his eyes.

I want to emphasize – it may sound like a cliché – Jesus can heal your body today. You can receive your healing now and know regardless of the circumstances that Jesus Christ can heal your body just like he healed the blind man. This was not circumstantial evidence as the Pharisees perceived it to be. This was the hand of the almighty God working a healing miracle through His Son Jesus Christ. If you can receive this message as the true gospel, then you can receive your healing miracle today.

A Twist of Fate

Romans 8:26-30/ Romans 8:28

"And we know that all things work together for good to those who love God, to those who are the called according to His purpose." (Romans 8:28 NKJV)

When I have to preach, the Holy Spirit often gives me a scripture, a title, or illustrations. Sometimes he wakes me up in the middle of the night or the early morning with the word manifested into my heart and I reach over grab my pen jot down a few words and go back to sleep. This is the exact thing that happened to me in relation to this sermon. I jotted down the title and then later the Holy Spirit gave me these words:

> Humpty Dumpty sat on a wall,
> Humpty Dumpty had a great fall.
> All the king's horses and all the king's men
> Couldn't put Humpty together again.

How many of you remember this very familiar nursery rhyme? The rhyme was first printed in 1810. It describes a short and clumsy person who was sitting on a wall and had a great fall. Humpty Dumpty was portrayed as an egg. He obviously was not a boiled egg because none of the pieces could be put back together. If you think about it, once you drop an egg on the floor, it cracks and the yolk splatters on the ground. It's hard to gather up a raw egg and pick it up once it is on the floor. If a clumsy man fall's off a wall, he would not be irreparably damaged but an egg would be. I must confess that the title of this message made me question the Lord about these illustrations.

The title of this message is *A Twist of Fate*. The word "fate" is described as something that unavoidably befalls a person. The word fate is something predetermined and inescapable. The word fate can also be described as your overall circumstances or conditions in life (including everything that happens to you). For example are you a victim of your circumstances? Do you deserve a better fate? Are you down on your luck? Some synonyms of the word "fate" include luck, destiny, and doom.

Sometimes your fate can be twisted. What does this actually mean? You can plan or look for an expected result but the circumstances change. For example, you can plan a wonderful wedding and expect a wonderful marriage, but it ends in divorce. If you expect the best for your children and they refuse to obey you, they may end up incarcerated or they may flunk out of school. They may not have any goals or ambitions. What if you plan to get a promotion on your job and you are overlooked. What if you quit your job to start your own company and the business fails. What if your relationships with your friends are in disarray and you fail to discuss the problems but feel hurt and saddened all the time. These are some examples of twisted fate. Another way to describe twisted fate is when things don't work out the way you thought they would. Twisted Fate can cause you to have serious issues, if you do not deal with them. For example, it may lower yourself esteem, or you may have an inferiority complex. You may have emotional highs and lows. You may not be able to acknowledge your gifts and talents because you have been wounded by pass experiences.

A Few Minutes With God

What do you do when all of your dreams have been crushed? The Bible says in Romans 8:28, "And we know that all things work together for good to those who love God, to those who are the called according to His purpose." It is an interesting revelation between the Bible and Humpty Dumpty. When Humpty Dumpty fell off of the wall, no one could put him back together again. It said that all the king's horses and all the king's men couldn't put Humpty together again. Although this is a popular nursery rhyme that we learned as children, it states that once Humpty Dumpty fell off the wall there was no help for him. It was a tragedy. No one could help him.

However, the Apostle Paul says that, "All things work together for good" (Romans 8:28). There are some criteria for all things to work together:

1. Sometimes you may have good times and sometimes you may have bad times but God is always at work for your good.
2. The promise is for "those who love God." You must be born again and love God and not be rebellious for things to work together for your good.
3. For things to work together for your good, it means God is dealing with both the spiritual and the eternal so that you may glorify God.

Let's repeat the verse again. Romans 8:28 says, "And we know that all things work together for good to those who love God, to those who are the called according to His purpose." The NIV version states this scripture a little differently. It says, "And we know that in all things God works for the good of those who love him, who have been called according to his purpose." In other words, God is working things out for your good, if you love him. He is working things out for your good for those who are called according to His purpose. When you are called by God he sends you a summons just like in the court of law. He invites you to be one of his ambassadors for the kingdom. He first invites you to become a child of God. He invites you to have a personal relationship with Him. He invites you to become a part of the body of Christ. Once you become a part of the body of Christ, He can deliver you from past hurts, from a broken heart, from defeats, failures and mistakes because He is the giver of life, He is our redeemer, He is the king of kings and the Lord of Lords. Jesus died for our sins and He arose three days later to conquer death, hell and the grave. It is your choice to follow Him. It is your choice to surrender your life to Him. It is your choice to exalt Him, to worship Him and adore Him. If you don't take time with the Master, you will never reach your potential. You will never fulfill your dreams. You will never know what God's desire for your life will be. You will never know the will of God for your life.

From my own personal experience, I would say that my life in some ways has been a twist of fate but when I accepted Jesus as my Personal Savior the road that I was headed down, a road of self destruction and self sabotage the Lord sent someone to me. In 1986, shortly after my divorce, I met a woman who became a significant part of my life. Although I wrestled with my new-found friend telling her that I went to church and that I was baptized at twelve years old, I did not know the significance of having a personal relationship with Jesus Christ until we prayed together and I accepted Jesus as my Personal Savior. Jesus can interrupt your life with divine appointments. Since that day I made a u-turn to follow Jesus, sometimes I still make mistakes but I trust him with my whole heart and my whole life. Sometimes we have to take a detour to get to the right road. Once you are on the right road Jesus will lead you and guide you by the Holy Spirit. He is the comforter. He is your guide. He will teach you about things to come. Surrender your whole life to Him because He is our Savior.

Let us reflect on the life of Joseph which is found in Genesis 37. He was hated by his brothers because he was his father's favorite son. He also had two dreams that made him appear to be arrogant because he would be the ruler over his brothers and even his parents.

Joseph's brothers plotted to kill him but instead they sold him into slavery to a group of Midianites. Joseph eventually became the ruler over Egypt under Pharoah. He was second in command. During the seven years of abundance, Egypt had an abundance of grain. During the seven years of famine the whole land was without food except Egypt. Joseph was able to sell grain to the Egyptians. All the countries came to Egypt to buy grain. Joseph's family eventually came to Egypt to live with him because of the famine.

In Genesis 50, Joseph reassures his brothers, after their father Jacob dies that he did not have a grudge against them even though they treated him so badly. Joseph father left instructions before he died asking him to forgive his brothers for treating him so badly. Joseph cried and his brothers threw themselves before him and said that they would be his slaves. Then Joseph said to them, "Do not be afraid, for am I in the place of God? But as for you, you meant evil against me; but God meant it for good, in order to bring it about as it is this day, to save many people alive. Now therefore, do not be afraid; I will provide for you and your little ones." And he comforted them and spoke kindly to them" (Genesis 50:19-21).

A Few Minutes With God

This was a twist of fate in a positive way. Joseph was a slave who rose to prominence. The Bible says, "And we know that all things work together for good to those who love God, to those who are the called according to His purpose" (Romans 8:28). Regardless of your circumstances, God is working it out for your good.

Humpty Dumpty was unable to get up after he fell off of the wall. But the Bible says in Proverbs 24:16 NIV, "For though a righteous man falls seven times he rises again, but the wicked are brought down by calamity." KJV says, "For a just man falleth seven times, and riseth up again: but the wicked shall fall into mischief."

Who are you? Are you like Humpty Dumpty? Have you had a great fall and feel like you can't be put back together? Donnie McClurkin has a song called "We Fall Down." The verse says "We fall down but we get up, a saint is just a sinner who falls down and got up."

What about the walls in your life? The walls of iniquity, the walls of despair, the walls of hopelessness, the walls of depression, the walls of anxiety, the walls of fear, the walls of damnation, the walls of shame, the walls of defeat. Do you have these walls because of twisted fate? I've got good news. If you are on any of these walls, Jesus is right here today to catch you when you fall. When you fall you will fall into the grace and mercy of a loving God. He will pick you up. Jesus will pick you up and put you back together again. Then you will be able to know about the walls of faith, the walls of love, the walls of hope, the walls of peace, the walls of joy, the walls of forgiveness. And whatever your problem is Jesus will fix it because "We know that all things work together for good to those who love God, to those who are the called according to His purpose" (Romans 8:28).

The Nature of your Inheritance

2Peter 1:1-11/2Peter 1:4

"By which have been given to us exceedingly great and precious promises, that through these you may be partakers of the divine nature, having escaped the corruption that is in the world through lust." (2Peter 1:4 NKJV)

As you probe the scriptures you will discover the nature of your inheritance as it relates to your identity in Christ. By the end of this message you should be able to analyze your own identity, whether it is sinfulness or holiness. There may be something inside you that is holding you back from complete purification or sanctification as it relates to your personal relationship with the Lord. Peter tackles the subject of divine nature very clearly in order to guide Christians or prompt them to become mature Christians.

When you are born again you inherit the nature of Christ, but the Bible reads in 1Peter 2:1-3, "Therefore, laying aside all malice, all deceit, hypocrisy, envy, and all evil speaking, as new born babes, desire the pure milk of the word, that you may grow thereby, if indeed you have tasted that the Lord is gracious."

Today, my task is to feed you spiritual food and that can only come from the word of God by the revelation of the Holy Spirit. When you sit down to eat a meal whether its breakfast, lunch, or dinner, you expect to be satisfied and to get full. That is why we so often go out to restaurants, whether it's fast food or fine dining. We often order the super size meals because we want to get full and we want to enjoy a variety of foods. However, in reality, food scientist say that it actually takes about 20 minutes before your brain recognizes that your stomach is full. Many people, including myself, may go back for seconds or even thirds until we over indulge.

The purpose of this message is to feed your spirit so that it may be satisfied with the word of God.

When Nicodemus spoke to Jesus about the born again experience, he misunderstood the nature of the experience. He assumed that Jesus was speaking of the physical rather than the spiritual. That's why Nicodemus asked Jesus the question, "How can a man be born when he is old? Can he enter a second time into his mother's womb and be born?" (John 3:4). It seemed to be a logical question in the mind of Nicodemus. Jesus answered him saying, "Unless one is born of water and the Spirit, he cannot enter the kingdom of God. That which is born of the flesh is flesh, and that which is born of the Spirit is spirit." (John 3:5-8).

Have you investigated the scriptures and asked yourself the question, what is the nature of Jesus Christ? First, He was without sin. When we are born again Jesus forgives us our sins. However, there are still some people in the body of Christ who still have carnal minds. The Bible states in Romans 8:5-11:

> For those who live according to the flesh set their minds on the things of the flesh, but those who live according to the Spirit, the things of the Spirit. For to be carnally minded is death, but to be spiritually

minded is life and peace. Because the carnal mind is enmity against God; for it is not subject to the law of God, nor indeed can be. So then, those who are in the flesh cannot please God.

But you are not in the flesh but in the Spirit, if indeed the Spirit of God dwells in you. Now if anyone does not have the Spirit of Christ, he is not His. And if Christ is in you, the body is dead because of sin, but the Spirit is life because of righteousness. But if the Spirit of Him who raised Jesus from the dead dwells in you, He who raised Christ from the dead will also give life to your mortal bodies through his Spirit who dwells in you.

I'm sure you are familiar with the scripture, Romans 3:23 which reads, "For all have sinned and fall short of the glory of God." Therefore, we must recognize that we all are sinners and that Jesus Christ died on the cross for our sins and forgave us our sins. When you are born again you repent of your sins, however if you continue to sin, this separates you from God. Sometimes we categorize sins. We place them in order from smallest to largest. For example, if you tell a little white lie, which seems not to hurt anyone, that's a small sin and you forget what the Bible says. It says God does not lie. On the other hand, if someone steals something or if someone commits murder, those sins are easily and quickly identified as large sins. The bottom line is that sin is sin and everyone who commits a sin and does not repent jeopardizes their relationship with Jesus Christ and jeopardizes their entrance into heaven.

Secondly, Jesus had compassion to heal those who were sick and those who had diseases. One illustration in the Bible said Jesus was moved with compassion. Matthew 9:36-38 reads, "But when He saw the multitudes, He was moved with compassion for them, because they were weary and scattered, like sheep having no shepherd. Then He said to His disciples, The harvest truly is plentiful, but the laborers are few. Therefore pray the Lord of the harvest to send out laborers into His harvest."

In my own interpretation or revelation, the word "compassion" means to have a strong desire to meet the needs of the person. In comparison, the definition on *dictionary.com* describes compassion as a "deep awareness of the suffering of another, coupled with the wish to relieve it." Several synonyms include "pity" and "sympathy."

When you are moved with compassion, the Bible says in James 1:27, "Pure and undefiled religion before God and the Father is this: to visit orphans and widows in their trouble, and to keep oneself unspotted from the world."

Remember the parable that Jesus tells of the Good Samaritan? I'm sure you know the story. To paraphrase it, in Luke 10:25-36, a young lawyer approached Jesus and asked him the question, "What shall I do to inherit eternal life?" Jesus answered him and said, "Did you read what is written in the law? The lawyer answered and said, you shall love the Lord your God with all your heart, with all your soul, with all your strength, and with all of your mind, and love your neighbor as yourself." Then Jesus replied, "That is right, do this and live." Then the lawyer, wanting to justify himself, said to Jesus, "who is my neighbor?" Jesus said, "There was a certain man going from Jerusalem to Jericho, who fell among thieves who left him half dead after they had stripped his clothes and wounded him. A priest came down the road. And when he saw him, he passed by on the other side. Next a Levite was also passing down the road and looked at the man and passed on the other side. But finally, a certain Samaritan, saw the man and was moved with compassion. He bandaged his wounds, pouring oil and wine; and put him on his animal, took him to an inn and took care of him. On the following day before the Good Samaritan departed, he took out two denarii, gave them to the innkeeper and told him to take care of him and if that was not enough money he would pay him when he comes back through the city." So Jesus asked the lawyer the question, "Which of these three was the neighbor?" He said, "He who showed mercy of him." Then Jesus said to him, "Go and do likewise."

I say to you today, even in this modern day world, go and do likewise. If you know someone who needs food, feed them. If you know someone who needs clothes or shelter, help them to fulfill their need. If someone needs a job, give them some advice and show them the way. If someone is sick, pray for them. If someone is lonely, become their friend and lead them to Jesus, who is a friend above every friend. I say to you today go and do likewise in the name of Our Lord and Savior Jesus Christ.

Let us turn to another characteristic, or nature, of Christ. The prophet Isaiah says in Isaiah 53:3-4, "He was despised and rejected by men, A Man of sorrows and acquainted with grief. And we hid, as it were, our faces from Him; He was despised, and we did not esteem Him. Surely He has borne our griefs And carried our sorrows." I want to specifically talk about the subject of rejection and grief. The Bible says that Jesus was "despised and rejected by men, A Man of sorrows and acquainted with grief."

Those few words "acquainted with grief" illuminated my mind as I was preparing this message. All of us are acquainted with grief at some point in our lives. It may be death of a loved one or friend. It may be disappointment with your children. It may be miscommunication with your spouse. It may be a job that is challenging. It may be disappointment in your own ability to be obedient to Jesus Christ. According to the Bible, Jesus Christ knows even the number of hairs on our head. Isaiah tells us He was acquainted with grief because he had the heavy burden of knowing our sins and of His coming death on the cross.

We must understand that Jesus did not come to earth in an elaborate fashion. He came as a servant to mankind. He came as an example to the world that our human nature or our human flesh must be regenerated. In other words, we must be born again.

Another characteristic of Jesus is light. Jesus said in John 8:12, "I am the light of the world. He who follows Me shall not walk in darkness, but have the light of life." In Matthew 5:14-16, Jesus explains, "You are the light of the world. A city that is set on a hill cannot be hidden. Nor do they light a lamp and put it under a basket, but on a lampstand, and it gives light to all who are in the house. Let your light so shine before men, that they may see your good works and glorify your Father in heaven."

Jesus Christ is the light of the world and there is no darkness in Him. If you imagine yourself as a light, you will become brighter and brighter as you continuously surrender to the gifts and callings in your life. As you let your light shine among your friends, let your light shine among your family. Let your light shine among your coworkers, and let your light shine as you fellowship with those who are in the faith. The Bible states, "But be doers of the word and not hearers only" (James 1:22). If you do the Lord's will in spreading the gospel, by being obedient to the word, forgiving others, and being a servant then your light will shine, and the Lord will say, "Well done, good and faithful servant; you have been faithful over a few things, I will make you ruler over many things. Enter into the joy of the Lord" (Matthew 25:23).

The last characteristics of Jesus that I want to discuss is found in John 14:6. Jesus said, "I am the way, the truth, and the life. No one comes to the Father except through Me." In other words, there is no other way to enter the kingdom of God. There is no other way to inherit eternal life except through accepting Jesus as your Personal Savior. He is the way. He is the only way. There is no other name above except the name of Jesus.

Your inheritance comes when you partake of the divine nature. When you study and analyze the works and characteristics of Jesus Christ and when you understand His nature, then you can become imitators of Christ. Let us just recap for a moment. First Jesus was without sin. He was compassionate. He was rejected and acquainted with grief. He is the light of the world and finally He is the way the truth and the life. Take a look at your inheritance. Take a look at yourself and see if you see Christ's divine nature within yourself. If your nature is not like Christ's nature, then you need to do some self-searching, some examining, and some repenting so that you can receive your inheritance.

Journey of A Lost man

Matthew 18:10-14/Matthew 18:11

"For the Son of Man has come to save that which was lost"
(Matthew 18:11 NKJV)

When Jesus teaches the disciples the parable of the lost sheep, He describes a man who has one hundred sheep, but one of them goes astray. He decides to go to look for the sheep that wondered off. If the man finds the stray sheep, he should rejoice more of him than over the ninety-nine sheep. Then Jesus says, "For the Son of Man has come to save that which was lost" (Matthew 18:11).

The significance of this statement is true even today. Jesus saves those who are lost. Who are the lost? The lost are those who do not know Jesus Christ as their Personal Savior.

We live in a world with no boundaries. Anything goes. Yet, the bible speaks of the lost. Jesus said as he sent out the twelve disciples:

> Do not go into the way of the Gentiles, and do not enter a city of the Samaritans. But go rather to the lost sheep of the house of Israel. And as you go, preach, saying, "The kingdom of heaven is at hand." Heal the sick, cleanse the lepers, raise the dead, cast

out demons. Freely you have received, freely give. Provide neither gold nor silver nor copper in your money belts, nor bag for your journey, nor two tunics, nor sandals, nor staff; for a worker is worthy of his food.

Now whatever city or town you enter, inquire who in it is worthy, and stay there till you go out. And when you go into a household, greet it. If the household is worthy, let your peace come upon it. But if it is not worthy, let your peace return to you. And whoever will not receive you nor hear your words, when you depart from that house or city, shake off the dust from your feet. Assuredly, I say to you, it will be more tolerable for the land of Sodom and Gomorrah in the day of judgment than for that city (Matthew 10:5-15).

Hear the words of the Lord: "But go rather to the lost sheep of the house of Israel" (Matthew 10:6). Who are the lost sheep? The Jews called anyone who was not a Jew, a Gentile. Jesus gave the disciples the assignment to go to the lost sheep of the house of Israel.

If you are lost, Jesus is concerned about you. He is the only way to God. It is only through Jesus Christ that you can receive the gift of eternal life. If you are lost today, Jesus wants to give you the gift of life. Jesus wants you to know the power of the Holy Spirit. If you are lost, Jesus wants to reveal the living word of God to you. Once you are saved, He will reveal His purpose and His plans to you.

Do you remember the familiar scriptures John 3:16-17? Jesus said, "For God so loved the world that He gave His only begotten Son, that whoever believes in Him should not perish but have everlasting life. For God did not send His Son into the world to condemn the world, but that the world through Him might be saved."

Many reject Jesus today, just as they rejected Him 2000 years ago. Many challenge man's wisdom because he believes in a God that he cannot see. Do you look at man and his mistakes and then want to deny Christ? If you are lost, then you bare all of your burdens. If you do not understand the purpose of Jesus' sacrifice, then you may not understand the significance of salvation. It is necessary to have two births in your lifetime: your physical birth, the day that you were born, and the new birth, the day you were born again. The new birth places you in the Body of Christ.

A lost man does not know Jesus or understand the importance of the kingdom. But Jesus says, "Ask, and it will be given to you; seek, and you will find; knock, and it will be opened to you. For everyone who asks receives, and he who seeks finds, and to him who knocks it will be opened" (Matthew 7:7-8).

Why do some people stray away from God? Is there someone lost in your family? Is someone lost on your job? Is someone lost in your neighborhood? Some people stray away because they are looking for something instant. Salvation is free and it is a gift. However the Bible says that you need to "work out your own salvation with fear and trembling; for it is God who works in you both to will and to do for His good pleasure" (Philippians 2:12). This message is for those who are lost. It's amazing that we can put time and money into education for a higher degree, yet, some fail to seek the Living Savior, Jesus Christ.

Have you ever seen a newborn baby? He cannot do anything for himself. He drinks milk, and then he is spoon-fed baby food. As he grows, he develops teeth, and is able to eat solid food. When you are first born again, you need to find somebody to feed you, a church, a Bible study, Sunday school. If you want to know the ABC's of life, then you must know He is not just alive, but He lives in you.

Once you have received Jesus Christ as your Personal Savior, you will start a new journey. Then, you must put your priorities in order. "But seek first the kingdom of God and His righteousness, and all these things shall be added to you" (Matthew 6:33). The journey of a lost man is not the will of God. It is God's desire through Jesus Christ that everyone will be saved. To do the will of God, you must be submissive, you must obey God's word and you must yield to his perfect will. The journey of a lost man can be converted just like Paul on the Damascus Road. If you do not know Jesus as your Personal Savior, I believe this is a great day to get saved. Salvation. I always call it the best free gift anywhere.

Sealed With A Kiss

Matthew 26:45-49/ Matthew 26:48

"Now His betrayer had given them a sign, saying, 'Whomever I kiss, He is the One; seize Him.'"(Matthew 26:48 NKJV)

The kiss is an expression of respect, friendliness, or love. The people of the Western world use this as a form of expression, but the Japanese and Chinese seldom do. Polynesians express affection by rubbing their noses, and the Samoans sniff. Some people pay homage to their rulers by kissing the ground on which they walk.

The custom of kissing the foot or the hand of political or religious rulers dates from ancient times. The early Christians took the custom of kissing from the Romans and made it a part of the ceremony of their religion. It is known as the kiss of peace in the Roman Catholic and Eastern Orthodox Church. Roman Catholics kiss the pope's ring to show reverence. The kiss probably did not become widespread until the A.D. 500's.

Let us take a moment to examine the man called Judas Iscariot, the man who betrayed Jesus with a kiss. Judas was a man who was called by Jesus to be one of his disciples; a man who kissed the Messiah and also kissed death at the same time. The Bible says that it would have been better if Judas Iscariot had not been born. When Jesus called the twelve disciples one by one. He sent them forth and commanded them saying, "Go not into the way of the Gentiles, and into any city of the Samaritans enter ye not: But go rather to the lost sheep of Israel" (Matthew 10:5-6 KJV). This is important to know because it shows that Jesus did not treat Judas any differently than he treated the other eleven disciples. In fact, Judas was the treasurer for the group. Judas, who was the son of Simon, was an innocent man until he betrayed Jesus. You might ask why Jesus chose Judas to be one of the disciples when he knew that he would betray him. Let me set the scene for you. In Matthew 26:2 KJV, Jesus says to his disciples, "Ye know that after two days is the feast of the Passover and the Son of man is betrayed to be crucified."

Jesus told the disciples to "Go into the city to a certain man, and say to him, 'The Teacher says, "My time is at hand; I will keep the Passover at your house with My disciples."'" So the disciples did as Jesus had directed them; and they prepared the Passover. When evening had come, He sat down with the twelve. Now as they were eating, He said, "Assuredly, I say to you, one of you will betray Me." And they were exceedingly sorrowful, and each of them said to Him, "Lord, is it I?" He answered and said, "He who dipped his hand with Me in the dish will betray Me." "The Son of Man indeed goes just as it is written of Him, but woe to that man by whom the Son of Man is betrayed! It would have been good for that man if he had not been born." Then Judas, who was betraying Him, answered and said, "Rabbi, is it I?" He said to him, "You have said it" (Matthew 26:18-25 NKJV).

"Then one of the twelve, called Judas Iscariot, went unto the chief priests, And said unto them, 'What will ye give me, and I will deliver him unto you?' And they covenanted with him for thirty pieces of silver. And from that time he sought opportunity to betray him" (Matthew 26:14-16 KJV). The scene in the Garden of

Gethsemane found Jesus and the disciples at the Mount of Olives. He told the disciples to pray that temptation may not enter into them. Jesus told the disciples to watch and pray so that they would not enter into temptation. However, the disciples kept falling asleep. Jesus prayed, "O My Father, if it is possible, let this cup pass from Me; nevertheless, not as I will, but as You will" (Matthew 26:39 NKJV).

And while Jesus was still speaking, Judas appeared with a detachment of troops and officers from the chief priest and the Pharisees came with torches, and weapons. Judas drew near to Jesus to kiss Him. But Jesus said to him, "Judas, are you betraying the Son of Man with a kiss?" (Luke 22:48 NKJV).

Isn't it ironic that Judas would betray Jesus with a kiss? The very thing that people do to show love and affection. Judas, who was one of the twelve, had told the priest and the Pharisees that there would be a sign. The sign would be a kiss. Judas walked up to Jesus and said, "Greetings, Rabbi!" and kissed Him (Matthew 26:49 NKJV).

In that hour Jesus said to the multitudes, "Have you come out, as against a robber, with swords and clubs to take Me? I sat daily with you, teaching in the temple, and you did not seize Me. But all this was done that the Scriptures of the prophets might be fulfilled. Then all the disciples forsook Him and fled" (Matthew 26:55-56 NKJV). Jesus did not let a traitor stop Him from doing the will of His Father.

"Then Judas, His betrayer, seeing that He had been condemned, was remorseful and brought back the thirty pieces of silver to the chief priests and elders, saying, "I have sinned by betraying innocent blood." And they said, "What is that to us? You see to it!" Then he threw down the pieces of silver in the temple and departed, and went and hanged himself. But the chief priests took the silver pieces and said, "It is not lawful to put them into the treasury, because they are the price of blood." And they consulted together and bought with them the potter's field, to bury strangers in. Therefore that field has been called the Field of Blood to this day. Then was fulfilled what was spoken by Jeremiah the prophet, saying, "And they took the thirty pieces of silver, the value of Him who was priced, whom they of the children of Israel priced, "and gave them for the potter's field, as the Lord directed me" (Matthew 27:3-10 NKJV).

There are many mysteries about Judas, the disciple who betrayed Jesus. Why did he use a kiss, the very thing that people use to show love and affection? This man had one of the highest callings in the world, to be called a disciple of Christ. He didn't get second hand information. Judas was there when Jesus turned water into wine. He was there when Jesus healed the sick. He was there when Jesus raised the dead. He was there during the miracle of feeding the five thousand and still he betrayed Jesus. Such a tragic ending for a man with such high expectations.

Have you betrayed Jesus by thoughts, or words or your deeds? If you have betrayed Jesus in your heart, you need to repent today. You don't have to be like Judas who discovered too late that he had betrayed innocent blood. Don't die without confessing your sins to the Master. Judas sealed Jesus with a kiss. It was a kiss of death for Judas. Yet, the kiss is used to show love and affection. As a matter of fact, the best part of a wedding is when the minister says to the groom that you may kiss your bride! You should spend your lifetime sealing your mate and your children with a kiss. Judas failed to establish a personal relationship with Jesus Christ while Jesus was on earth. If you come to church, but neglect to ask Jesus to come into your heart and live inside you, then you have missed the purpose of going to church. Just like Judas, who was a disciple, missed his purpose for being on earth. Satan entered his heart and never left him. He never repented. But thank God we are not in this situation. Jesus died for our sins. The blood that he shed on Calvary was His redemptive blood. It is the blood for the dying. It is the blood for the broken hearted. In Him we have eternal life. In Him we have hope. When you seal someone with a kiss, make sure it is because the love of God is in your heart and let it not be to betray your brother or sister.

Sin, Sin, and More Sin

Judges 2:18-19/ Judges 2:11

"Then the children of Israel did evil in the sight of the Lord, and served The Baals" (Judges 2:11 NKJV)

In the old testament of the Bible, the book of Judges was named for the twelve judges who reigned from 1380-1050BC. God raised up these judges to lead and to govern their communities. However, the Bible says, in Judges 2:18-19:

> And when the Lord raised up judges for them, the Lord was with the judge and delivered them out of the hand of their enemies all the days of the judge; for the Lord was moved to pity by their groaning because of those who oppressed them and harassed them. And it came to pass, when the judge was dead, that they reverted and behaved more corruptly than their fathers, by following other gods, to serve them and bow down to them. They did not cease from their own doings nor from their stubborn way.

There is a phrase that was coined about the book of Judges called a Cycle of Sin. This Cycle lasted for 350 years. The pattern for the Cycle of Sin was sin, bondage, repentance, devotion, followed by sin and bondage again. For example, Israel serves the Lord. Next, Israel falls into sin and idolatry. Third Israel is enslaved.

Fourth, Israel calls out to the Lord. Fifth, God raises up a Judge. Sixth, Israel is delivered. Then the cycle begins again or repeats itself after the appointment of each judge. The people were so caught up in worshiping idols and false gods that they disobeyed God. Therefore, the Lord continued to raise up Judges to accomplish His task; but the people were still disobedient.

The power of sin is often misplaced or misunderstood. In today's society, most people have some type of moral values, but the moral values or boundaries have been broadened and sometime they're just often overlooked. If you understand the significance of sin and how it can dominate your life, you might ask the question, how do I dispose of it? How do I eliminate sin? Or how do I get rid of sin?

First, you must understand the significance of this message. The Bible says in Judges 2:11:

> Then the children of Israel did evil in the sight of the Lord, and served the Baals; and they forsook the Lord God of their fathers, who had brought them out of the land of Egypt; and they followed other gods from among the gods of the people who were all around them; and they bowed down to them; and they provoked the Lord to anger. They forsook the Lord and served Baal and the Ashtoreths [Canaanite goddesses]. And the anger of the Lord was hot against Israel. So He delivered them into the hands of plunderers who despoiled them; and He sold them into the hands of their enemies all around, so that they could no longer stand before their enemies.

Wherever they went out, the hand of the Lord was against them for calamity, as the Lord had said, and as the Lord had sworn to them. And they were greatly distressed. Nevertheless, the Lord raised up judges who delivered them out of the hand of those who plundered them. Yet they would not listen to their judges, but they played the harlot with other gods, and bowed down to them. They turned quickly from the way in which their fathers walked, in obeying the commandments of the Lord; they did not do so (Judges 2:11-17).

Is your behavior a cycle of sin? Do you compromise your beliefs because of peer pressure or because of society's attitude about certain things? Are you a habitual sinner? The children of Israel had a problem. They could not stay on course because they served and bowed down to false gods. What is sin and how is it depicted in the modern world?

According to Christianity's beliefs and doctrines, which are found in the book of Genesis, sin entered the world during the temptation and fall of man. God created male as well as female in His image. God placed Adam in the Garden of Eden, caused him to fall asleep, took one of his ribs, made a woman, and brought her to him. The Bible states that Adam said: "This is now bone of my bones and flesh of my flesh; She shall be called Woman, Because she was taken out of Man. Therefore a man shall leave his father and mother and be joined to his wife, and they shall become one flesh. And they were both naked, the man and his wife, were not ashamed" (Genesis 2:23-25).

The temptation and the fall of man placed humanity in a precarious situation. God gave Adam and Eve a direct commandment. They could eat the fruit of every tree in the Garden of Eden except the tree of the knowledge of good and evil. If they were to eat the fruit of this tree, they would die. However, the serpent questioned Eve about God's commandment and challenged her to eat the fruit of the tree of knowledge. The serpent told her, that she would not die but would know the difference between good and evil. So Eve ate the fruit and gave it to her husband Adam to eat.

After eating the fruit, both Adam and Eve's eyes were opened and they realized they were naked. Each covered themselves with fig leaves. They heard the Lord walking and hid themselves among the trees. Then the Lord God called to Adam and said to him, "Where are you" (Genesis 3:9)? Adam told God that he had hid himself, because he was naked and afraid. And He said, "Who told you that you were naked? Have you eaten from the tree of which I commanded you that you should not eat?" Then the man said, "The woman whom You gave to be with me, she gave me of the tree, and I ate." And the Lord God said to the woman, What is this you have done?" The woman said, "The serpent deceived me, and I ate" (Genesis 3:11-13).

This is the foundation of original sin. Adam and Eve's disobedience changed the course of humanity's purpose, thereby, bringing into existence the sinful nature. Sin separates men from God. There are many scriptures in the Bible pertaining to sin. This is the reason Jesus came to earth. He came so that He could forgive us for our sins. Jesus understood the nature and origin of sin. In Revelations 2:7: "He who has an ear, let him hear what the Spirit says to the churches. To him who overcomes I will give to eat from the tree of life, which is in the midst of the Paradise of God."

The tree of knowledge that Adam and Eve ate from in the Garden of Eden is in the book of Genesis, the first book of the bible. However, in the book of Revelations, the last book of the bible, Jesus says, that the tree of life is found in the midst of the Paradise of God. I've never made the comparison before now, but here's my point: at the beginning of the bible in Genesis, there is the tree of knowledge. At the end in Revelation, there is the tree of life. One tree you might say was used as a test and the other was used to confirm everlasting life. God promises us everlasting life when we receive Jesus as our Personal Savior.

The Apostle Paul says, in the book of Romans, "For all have sinned and fall short of the glory of God" (Romans 3:23). Another scripture, 1 John 1:8-9 reads, "If we say that we have no sin, we deceive ourselves, and the truth is not in us. If we confess our sins, He is faithful and just to forgive us our sins and to cleanse us from unrighteousness. If we say that we have not sinned, we make Him a liar, and His word is not in us." The gospel of John 1:29 states, "The next day John saw Jesus coming toward him, and said, "Behold! The Lamb of God who takes away the sin of the world!" That was Jesus main purpose to free us from sin.

Now what about the sin cycle and how does it relate to your relationship with Jesus Christ? Have you repented of your sins? To repent means to turn away from your sins, to feel remorse or sorrow for your sins, to change for the better after acknowledging your sins. Remember, John the Baptist said, "Repent, for the kingdom of heaven is at hand" (Matthew 3:2).

Then in Matthew 3:11 John the Baptist says, "I indeed baptize you with water unto repentance, but He who is coming after me is mightier than I, whose sandals I am not worthy to carry. He will baptize you with the Holy Spirit and fire."

Are you caught up in a cycle of sin like the children of Israel? If you are, I suggest that you determine what your relationship is with Jesus Christ. And seek Him to unravel the sin in your life.

There's No Storm Without Jesus

Luke 8:22-25/ Luke 8:23

"But as they sailed He fell asleep. And a windstorm came down on the lake, and they were filling with water, and were in jeopardy." (Luke 8:23 NKJV)

I want to speak to you about a serious matter. Hurricane season lasts from June to November in Florida. We are bombarded with information about what to do if a hurricane comes to this area. We are reminded over and over again to prepare for a hurricane.

Imagine yourself in this situation with Jesus and His disciples. To paraphrase, Jesus got into the boat with the disciples and asked them to cross over to the other side of the lake as they sailed. Jesus fell asleep and a windstorm arose and the disciples were afraid that they would drown. The boat was filling up with water and they felt that their lives were in jeopardy. They awoke Jesus because they were afraid that the boat would sink. After Jesus awoke, He rebuked the wind and the raging waters and they became calm. He asked the disciples, "Where is your faith?" The Bible says that the disciples marveled saying, "Who can this be?" (Luke 8:25). Jesus commanded, and still commands that the winds and the waters obey Him.

Many of you are probably familiar with the long running TV Show "The Love Boat." Well this boat in some ways was just like the Love Boat. When something happened on the ship, they always looked for the Captain to solve the problem or deal with the circumstances. Even though Jesus was asleep, they woke Him to take care of the situation. They felt that Jesus was the answer to the storm. The disciples depended on Him to calm the storm.

The word storm is also used in relation to people and their circumstances. These types of storms are not necessarily predictable. There are people who have had accidents. There are people who are sick. There are people who are depressed, lonely, and sad. There are people who have financial debt. There are people who are homeless, or on drugs or alcohol. And then there are those who have children that they cannot control. Someone may have died suddenly or unexpectedly in your family. These are simply the storms of life. I still continue to say that the world has no boundaries, anything goes. Yet, we are forced many times, through circumstances and situations in our lives, to call on Jesus. We are forced to wake Him. In the midst of your storms, Jesus is always on the scene. Jesus says, "I will never leave you nor forsake you" (Hebrews 13:5). He reinforces this by saying, "I am the Alpha and the Omega, the Beginning and the End" (Revelation 1:8). He says, "I am the resurrection and the life. He who believes in Me, though he may die, he shall live. And whoever lives and believes in Me shall never die" (John 11:25-26).

A storm, sometimes, is like an accident waiting to happen. The only way that you can get through a storm is to have faith in Jesus Christ. Remember Jesus asked the disciples, "Where is your faith?" They were sitting in the boat with Jesus and yet they still panicked and woke their Master up shouting, "Master, Master, we are perishing!" (Luke 8:24)

A Few Minutes With God

You may be on your bed of affliction today. You may be a bag of emotions, without a job, homeless, in financial debt, without a friend, or you may be in a bad relationship. Your children may be on drugs or in a gang, but it's not over yet. I'm asking you the same question that Jesus asked the disciples, "Where is your faith?" The Bible reads, "But without faith it is impossible to please Him, for he who comes to God must believe that He is, and that He is a rewarder of those who diligently seek Him" (Hebrews 11:6).

If you have ever seen a 3D picture, you know that you can see three sides. This illustration can be used in reference to the Trinity. The word Trinity refers to God the Father, Jesus His Son, and the Holy Spirit. God created the world. Jesus, His Son, died for our sins, and the Holy Spirit lives within us once we are born again. Why is this significant? Jesus was physically on the boat with the disciples. He was there on earth as a human being. They saw Jesus. They knew Jesus. They were Jesus' followers. They were His disciples. Yet, we find them marveling at the fact that He was able to calm the storm.

The Bible says, that "God has dealt to each one a measure of faith" (Romans 12:3). In other words, your faith can increase and decrease. The Apostle Paul speaks about this in relation to spiritual gifts. My point is that the disciples did not have faith enough to believe that the storm would cease without waking Jesus. They panicked. They did not know how to calm the storm themselves.

The bible story reminds us that Jesus is present in the midst of the storm. There Is No Storm Without Jesus. He was there on the boat with the disciples physically. He is here today. You cannot see Him or touch Him, but He is here today moving by the Holy Spirit.

The cross gives you access to Jesus Christ. In other words, Jesus is accessible through the cross. When we understand the purpose of the cross, then we can begin to comprehend the significance of the cross. Jesus died on the cross so that you may have eternal life. Jesus died on the cross so that you may have an abundant life. Jesus died on the cross so that your sins may be forgiven. When you receive Him as your Personal Savior, then the messages of God through Jesus Christ become prevalent in your life.

There Is No Storm Without Jesus. So, I want you to count your blessings. Increase your faith knowing that Jesus Christ is with you to calm your storms. The Holy Spirit is here to guide you through the paths of righteousness. The storms in your life can be calmed right now, today.

You may be thinking ok, how do I calm the storms in my life? First, believe in Jesus Christ. Then obey His commandments. Communicate with God through prayer. Meditate in the word of God. Become a disciple of Jesus Christ. Jesus said, "If you abide in My word, you are My disciples indeed. And you shall know the truth, and the truth shall make you free" (John 8:31-32).

You may have to cry out to Jesus, just like the disciples yelled, "Master, Master, we are perishing." If you are perishing, if you are in the midst of a storm today, remember, There Is No Storm Without Jesus. I want you to say that to yourself right now: There Is No Storm Without Jesus. This truly is a simple message, but a powerful one because you must know that Jesus will calm the storms in your life. And you must believe that There Is No Storm Without Jesus.

The Formula For Life

Matthew 24:26-35/ Matthew 24:35

"Heaven and earth shall pass away, but my words shall not pass away." (Matthew 24:35 KJV)

As I expound on the word of God, I am going to identify the Formula for Life. The setting for Matthew 24 is Jesus sitting up on the Mount of Olives. As he sat, the disciples came to him and wanted to know the sign of His coming and when the end of the world would come. Jesus said to the disciples that many would come saying that, "I am the Christ" (Matthew 24:5). They will deceive many, and you will hear of wars and rumors of wars, but this will not be the end of the world. Nation will rise against nation. There will be famines and earthquakes. These will be the beginning of sorrows, but the end will not come yet. Jesus also tells us to remember that you may be killed and hated for His name sake. Many false prophets will rise up and many will be deceived. The love of many will grow cold because lawlessness will abound, but those who endure to the end shall be saved.

These illustrations give a synopsis of Jesus' teaching on the Mount of Olives. The Bible also addresses the fact that we may not know what we are doing when Christ comes back. To paraphrase Matthew 18, Jesus says if you are on the roof of the house. Don't go back inside of your house. Those who are in the field don't go back to get your clothes. He also says to pray that he does not come back on the Sabbath because there will be great tribulation on that day. The parable of the fig tree is found in Matthew 24:32-35. The Bible says, "When his branch is yet tender, and putteth forth leaves, ye know that summer is nigh: So likewise ye, when ye shall see all these things, know that it is near, even at the doors. Verily I say unto you, This generation shall not pass, till all these things be fulfilled. Heaven and earth shall pass away, but my words shall not pass away." If you understand the power of the word of God, you will understand the Formula for Life. Ask yourself this question, do I know the Formula for Life?

If you understand the power of formulas, for example in math and science problems, you will get the correct answer by placing some numbers into the formulas and then performing the operation. I understand this well because I have a chemistry degree from Bethune-Cookman University. I had to take classes not only in chemistry but, in advanced math. I'm sure some of you have taken algebra. There are all types of formulas that you must learn to successfully complete the course. According to *dictionary.com*, a formula is any fixed or conventional method for doing something. For example, there is a formula in algebra called the Pythagorean Theorem. How many of you remember the formula for the Pythagorean Theorem? The formula is in relation to a triangle. If A and B are the length of the legs, and C is the length of the hypotenuse, which is the longest side of the right triangle ABC. Then A squared + B squared = C squared. Now let me make this clear: I am not here to teach math. I believe this is a logical point to help you understand the Formula for Life.

There is a rule for everything under the sun. If my phone number was 555-4444 and you dialed 444-5555, I will never answer the phone because that's not my number! We are always told that we need to call on Jesus and He will answer prayer. There are instructions in the Bible about how to pray. For instance in Matthew 18:20, Jesus says, "For where two or three are gathered together in my name, there am I in the midst of them." The Apostle Paul says in 1Thessalonians 5:17 to "Pray without ceasing." He also declares in Romans 8:26:

> Likewise the Spirit also helpeth our infirmities: for we know not what we should pray for as we ought: but the Spirit itself maketh intercession for us with groanings which cannot be uttered. And he that searcheth the hearts knoweth what is the mind of the Spirit, because he maketh intercession for the saints according to the will of God. And we know that all things work together for good to them that love God, to them who are the called according to his purpose.

The Holy Spirit prays with you and for you according to the will of God. You don't have to face your problems alone. Whatever your situation Jesus said, "I will never leave thee, nor forsake thee" (Hebrews 13:5). Jesus Christ the same yesterday, and today, and forever" (Hebrews 13:8). Now do you understand the power of the word of God? Jesus Christ is the same yesterday, today and forever.

If you accept these scriptures as the truth, then you can receive the gospel as good news. Someone today ought to be healed by the power of God. Someone today ought to be saved, and filled with the Holy Ghost. Somebody ought to be delivered because the word of God is true.

A Few Minutes With God

God will meet your needs whether they are spiritual, emotional, or financial. If you believe that Jesus is the same yesterday, today, and forever and that the Bible is true and authentic, and that Jesus really lives. Then why aren't you placing your priorities in order? The Bible says "But seek ye first the kingdom of God, and his righteousness: and all these things shall be added unto you" (Matthew 6:33). We put our families, our jobs, our marriages, our children, our hobbies, and even church work before God. I am *not* advocating that you not work in the church. Jesus said, "The harvest truly is plenteous, but the laborers are few; Pray ye therefore the Lord of the harvest, that he will send forth laborers into his harvest" (Matthew 9:37-38).

Your relationship with Jesus Christ should be your first priority. Because didn't He sacrifice His life for you? Didn't He die on the cross for you? Didn't He shed His precious blood for you? Didn't He forgive your sins? Didn't he promise to give you eternal life? What more does Jesus have to do to get your attention?

When you live an unbalanced life, you are not only cheating God, but you're cheating yourself. Even in the First chapter of John it states, "In the beginning was the Word, and the Word was with God and the Word was God. The same was in the beginning with God." Later John 1:14 reads, "And the Word was made flesh, and dwelt among us, (and we beheld his glory, the glory as of the only begotten of the Father,) full of grace and truth."

What do these words really mean? I always say that Jesus came on earth to teach us how to live. He was the perfect teacher in Jesus' life we see how God thinks and therefore how we should think. If you need a role model, you should study the life of Jesus.

A Few Minutes With God

You might say friends have forsaken me. Mother and Father have forsaken me, my spouse has forsaken me, but Jesus Christ declares, "I am Alpha and Omega, the beginning and the end, the first and the last" (Revelation 22:13). The word of God says that, "Heaven and earth shall pass away, but my words shall not pass away" (Matthew 24:35). In other words, there are no words which are void in the Bible. They are all significant.

You must understand that when you become born again you are God's child. You need to act like God's child. You must renew your mind daily. You can't think or do what the world does and get to heaven. This is impossible. I remember one time when I was a teenager, I wanted to go to an event and I asked my dad if I could go. Well he said, "Arlena, you can't go." I responded, "But Daddy everybody else is going!" My parents were not really super strict but this time my dad said no. When I said that everybody else is going he said to me. "You are my child and you can't do what everyone else does." I tell this story to illustrate a point. When you're walking with Jesus you need to do what Jesus does and you need to say what Jesus says and you need to act like Jesus acts.

Apostle Paul states, "Be ye therefore followers of God, as dear children; And walk in love, as Christ also hath loved us, and hath given himself for us an offering and a sacrifice to God for a sweetsmelling savour" (Ephesians 5:1-2). You must commit yourself to a Christ-like life. Your life must be built on the solid rock of Jesus. He must be your cornerstone. He must be your anchor. We were created in his image to do his good works.

In this modern world, the technology is so advanced. You don't have to go to AAA any more to get directions to take a trip.

You can just go to your computer and pull up *Mapquest* and get the exact directions. Some cars have GPS that gives you the direction right in your vehicle. The voice that you hear is so real, it's almost scary.

If you want directions to live a holy life and to go to heaven, you need to talk to Jesus. Jesus said, "If ye continue in my word, then are ye my disciples indeed; And ye shall know the truth, and the truth shall make you free" (John 8:31-32). What a wonderful God we serve! Do you want to know The Formula for Life? It's really simple. It's simply the word of God.

Here Comes The Bride

Revelation 19:6-8/ Revelation 19:7

"Let us rejoice and be glad and give him glory! For the wedding of the lamb has come, and his bride has made herself ready."
(Revelation 19:7 NIV)

I'm going to be a little informal here. I want to tell you a story about how the Lord brought this particular sermon to my attention. I think this is important so that you can see how the Holy Spirit moves through ordinary people in ordinary circumstances.

On April 7, 1996, I did not attend the Easter Service. The reason that I was not at the service is because my mom and I were in Ft. Lauderdale. One of my cousins got married and on the Saturday before Easter Sunday we attended the wedding and the reception. On the next day my mother called her cousin, Louis. He's my cousin too but he is much older than my mother so we were raised to call him uncle. So my mom invited Uncle Louis to have brunch with us on Easter Sunday. We had to go pick him up and when we got to his house, he had this little computer bible. It's bigger than a calculator and smaller than a lap top computer. If you type in Psalm 100, the scripture verses will appear: "Make a joyful noise unto the Lord, all ye lands…"

You know when people tell a good joke, everybody's waiting for the punch line. So here is the punch line: Uncle Louis said to my mother, "I'm studying Revelation." After brunch, when Uncle Louis got out of the car, I got on my soapbox. Ya'll know what getting up on a soap box means, don't you? It's one step up from gossiping. I said, "Mama, Uncle Louis talking about he was studying the book of Revelation. I said preachers don't even preach out of the book of Revelation." I said, "Mama, when was the last time you heard a sermon on the book of Revelation?" You know what she did? She laughed, because she couldn't remember. I laughed too, because I couldn't remember any sermons even through seminary on the book of Revelation.

A week or ten days later, I was at the track walking. I took my CD player with me, so that I could listen to a little music while I'm walking. On that particular day, I was listening to the Brooklyn Tabernacle Choir. I was just walking and having a good time, until I got these thoughts that happened simultaneously and instantly. I realize that the Lord was giving me a sermon title in the book of Revelation. So I got home and I got my Bible and I started to read, and the Holy Spirit showed me the text which is found in Revelation 19:6-8. In verse 7, it says "And his bride has made herself ready."

Ladies if you've ever gotten married and decided to have a traditional wedding you know that there is a lot of preparation involved. You must choose your maid of honor and your bridesmaids. You need a flower girl and a ring bearer. You must decide where you will have the wedding, and where your reception will be. You need to send out invitations. And of course don't forget you must purchase a wedding gown.

If we examine the scriptures again, Revelation 19:7 says, "And his bride has made herself ready." If we compare this verse with a bride who has a traditional wedding you will find many similarities. The bride is making herself ready for her groom. But it is not the groom's day but all attention will be given to the bride because, it is her day, regardless of how handsome you think your groom appears.

When John speaks of the bride, he is not talking about the bride I've just described, but he is speaking about the church of our Lord and Savior Jesus Christ. The groom is Christ himself. We need to make ourselves ready for the coming of the Lord. Revelation 19:9 reads, "Blessed are those who are invited to the wedding supper of the Lamb!" Just like in a traditional wedding, you must be invited to the wedding supper. Christ, The Anointed One is coming back soon and we must be ready. When the bride walks down the aisle on her wedding day, all eyes are on her. The white wedding gown and the veil capture the hearts of everyone. While the bridal song "Here Comes The Bride" is being played by the musician everyone stands and looks in awe. The church body is the bride and when Jesus comes back, we will stand and look in awe at Him.

In 1Thessalonians 4:16-17, the Bible says:

For the Lord himself will come down from heaven, with a loud command, with the voice of the archangel and with the trumpet call of God, and the dead in Christ will rise first. After that, we who are still alive and are left will be caught up together with them in the clouds to meet the Lord in the air. And so we will be with the Lord forever.

If we look at verse 5:2 the scriptures says, "That the day of the Lord will come like a thief in the night."
John says once again "And his bride has made herself ready" (Revelation 19:7). The only way you can get ready is to examine

yourself. You need to go back to the basics. First thing you need to ask yourself: am I born again? There will be many people, who are good people who will not go to heaven. You might ask "Why do you say that, preacher?" The simple answer is that they will not accept Jesus as their Personal Savior. And we all know that the only way to the Father is through the Son.

Secondly, you need to obey God. I'm not just talking about the Ten Commandments. But I'm talking about the Bible in its entirety. It was written to show you how to live on earth. Jesus came on earth to show us how to live. You need to obey the Holy Spirit if he gives you revelation knowledge about your circumstances.

Third, we must remember to pray, the Bible says to "Pray without ceasing" (1 Thessalonians 5:17). The simple fact is: if you do not pray, there is no way that you can communicate with God. You should have the kind of relationship with Jesus Christ that you pray in the spirit and you pray with understanding. Before Jesus raised Lazarus from the dead, what did he do? He prayed, "Father, I thank you that you have heard me. I knew that you always hear me, but I said this for the benefit of the people standing here, that they may believe that you sent me" (John 11:41-42). Before He multiplied the loaves and the fish, He prayed. He went away from his apostles to pray even when the devil tempted him. He prayed anyway. Lastly on the cross, he prayed "Father forgive them, for they do not know what they are doing" (Luke 23:34).

See Jesus didn't have to pray, but He did. Jesus didn't have to obey, but He did. Jesus didn't have to walk the face of the earth 2000 years ago, but He did. Jesus didn't have to die on the cross for you, but He did. John illustrates the body of Christ perfectly. We are the bride, He is the groom. As you know marriage was designed by God. It is under the covenant. If I understand the scriptures correctly, when we are married on earth a new relationship is established. The bride and the groom become one. Flesh of my flesh and bone of my bone; until death do us part.

We are the church of the living Christ. If you are saved then you are in the church which is the bride of Christ. If you are not saved, then you are not in the church and you will not be caught up in the air with the Lord when he comes back. If you die unsaved, you will not rise when the trumpet sounds. But you will miss eternal life with Jesus Christ.

I realized that this is a short message, but it is my prayer, that when you hear the tune, "Here Comes The Bride," you will not only remember the bride that you are watching. But you will remember the bride of Christ. The words to "Here Comes The Bride" are "Here comes the bride all dressed in white thinks she's a lady but she's nothing but a child." You are a child of God if you are born again.

When you meet Jesus, you should be without blemish, you need to be pure and holy just like Revelation 19:7 says, "For the wedding of the Lamb has come and his bride has made herself ready."

Prepare For Landing, Destination Heaven

John 11:1-27/ John 11:25-26

Jesus said unto her, "I am the resurrection, and the life: he that believeth in me, though he were dead, yet shall he live: And whosoever liveth and believeth in me, shall never die."
(John 11:25-26 KJV)

There has always been a philosophical question about life after death. Those people who are not Christians often contemplate whether there's really a heaven or hell. Those who are Catholic even teach about purgatory, which is something like a holding place before the decision is made where your soul will go. In this modern day, death sometimes is taken lightly as if it will never happen to you. But death will knock at each of our doors. It doesn't matter whether you are rich or poor, Black or White, Hispanic or Asian. Death will come to all of us, sometimes, when we least suspect it.

Death has been on my mind lately because my godmother passed away on July 29, 2005 and also one of my cousins died that same year. Then Katrina happened. Looking at CNN and other news channels, we saw the faces that were worn by the storm and the President Bush was claiming "Help is on the way." But for many people in New Orleans, Mississippi and Alabama, death came before help arrived.

We usually hear these words at a funeral, "I am the resurrection, and the life: he that believeth in me, though he were dead, yet shall he live: and whosoever liveth and believeth in me shall never die" (John 11:25-26). Or these words: "For I know that my redeemer liveth, and that he shall stand at the latter day upon the earth: And though after my skin worms destroy this body, yet in my flesh shall I see God: Whom I shall see myself, and mine eyes shall behold and not another" (Job 19:25-27). Or these: "For we brought nothing into this world, and it is certain we can carry nothing out. The Lord gave, and the Lord hath taken away; blessed be the name of the Lord" (1 Timothy 6:7, Job 1:21).

I am not here to eulogize anyone because we are all alive, but I am here to help those who have not accepted Jesus Christ as their Personal Savior. I am here to urge you to accept Jesus today. It is imperative that you examine your lives so that as the old folks used to say, "When your ship comes in, you better be ready." President Bush might not get there in time. But if my ship comes in today, I know that I have King Jesus. I know to be absent from the body is to be present with the Lord. The Bible also says that to fear God is the beginning of wisdom. Knowing Jesus is my way through the pearly gates. The Bible says you must be born again. If you are not born again you can not see the kingdom of God.

The eleventh chapter of John describes the circumstances with Lazarus who was sick. He was the brother of Mary and Martha. When Lazarus became ill, they sent for Jesus. Jesus said, "This sickness is not unto death, but for the glory of God, that the Son of God, might be glorified thereby" (John 11:4). Jesus did not immediately go to Lazarus but stayed in the same place for two days. Lazarus was in the grave four days and Martha went to Jesus and said:

A Few Minutes With God

Lord if thou hadst been here, my brother had not died. But I know, that even now, whatsoever thou wilt ask of God, God will give it thee. Jesus saith unto her, "thy brother shall rise." Martha saith unto him, "I know that he shall rise again in the resurrection at the last day." Jesus said unto her, "I am the resurrection, and the life he that believeth in me, though he were dead, yet shall he live: And whosoever liveth and believeth in me shall never die (John 11:21-24).

Isn't this good news? The Bible says that when Jesus saw where Lazarus laid, "Jesus wept" (John 11:35). Jesus did not forget his mission. When the stone was rolled away. Jesus said, "Lazarus, come forth" (John 11:43).

To understand the significance of this, you must value life and Jesus Christ should not only be a part of your life but you must serve him everyday. You need to beware of Satan who is looking for whomever he may devour. September 11th caught all of us by surprise. Although there are hurricane warnings, they still take us by surprise. People are still homeless, jobless, and penniless, and some have gone on to their graves because of Katrina. The tsunami in Indonesia, the earthquake in Haiti. Nobody saw those coming.

I don't know about you, but knowing a little more about tragedy, I feel like I want a closer walk with God. I want to feel the presence of the Holy Spirit. Like the song "In the Garden" which says, "And He walks with me and He talks with me, And He tells me I am His own." I want to sing the familiar hymn "What a Friend We Have in Jesus." The lyrics say, "What a friend we have in Jesus,

All my sins and grief's to bear! What a privilege to carry everything to God in prayer." And I want to sing the song "Oh Happy Day" The words to this song are some of my favorites: "Oh happy day when Jesus washed my sins away!"

Have you talked to Jesus today? Do you feel the presence of the Holy Spirit? Are you alright with God? I am here as a concerned messenger for the Lord. I'm telling you, you need to get right with God. The Bible says, "Watch therefore, for ye know neither the day nor the hour wherein the Son of Man Cometh" (Matthew 25:13). We need to stay on guard.

In 1Corinthians 15:55-58, the Apostle Paul says:

> O death, where is thy sting? O grave, where is thy victory? The sting of death is sin; and the strength of sin is the law. But thanks be to God, which giveth us victory through our Lord Jesus Christ. Therefore, my beloved brethren, be ye stedfast, unmovable, always abounding in the work of the Lord, forasmuch as ye know that your labor is not in vain in the Lord.

Death has been defeated because Jesus Christ rose from the dead. Those who believe will be saved. The greatest gift that Jesus Christ has given to us is the gift of salvation. Salvation is free. You don't have to take out your credit card to get saved. You don't have to be a covenant partner with anyone's ministry to get saved. It's the best free gift in town and yet, there are people who refuse to come to Jesus. Yes, Jesus died on the cross, but that does not conclude the story. Just like Jesus said, "Lazarus come forth," the Bible says, "And the dead in Christ will rise first: Then we which are alive and remain shall be caught up together with them in the clouds, to meet the Lord in the air: and so shall we ever be in the Lord" (1 Thessalonians 4:16-17). Lazarus' sickness, which led to his demise, was so that the Son of God might be glorified. Somebody ought to Praise the Lord because you still have time to come to Jesus today.

I remember when K-Mart used to have those "blue light specials." You have to buy the item during that time to get the special price. You, who are children of God, should remember the blue light special when you come across someone who is unsaved. In your mind you should think Blue Light Special! This is the time to witness the goodness of God and lead someone to the Lord. Sundays are blue light special days. Someone will receive Jesus Christ as their Lord and Savior.

There is only one criterion to get to heaven and that is you must believe that Jesus is Christ and He died and arose from the dead. Romans 10:9-10 says, "That if thou shalt confess with thy mouth the Lord Jesus, and believe in thine heart that God hath raised him from the dead, thou shalt be saved. For with the heart man believeth unto righteousness; and with the mouth confession is made unto salvation."

The scriptures, according to Romans 8:5-12 NKJV read, "For the law of the Spirit of life in Christ Jesus has made me free from the law of sin and death" (Romans 8:2). The Bible tells us "For to be carnally minded is death, but to be spiritually minded is life and peace. Because the carnal mind is enmity against God; for it is not subject to the law of God, nor indeed can be. So then, those who are in the flesh cannot please God." The Apostle Paul goes on to say:

> But you are not in the flesh but in the Spirit, if indeed the Spirit of God dwells in you. Now if anyone does not have the Spirit of Christ, he is not His. And if Christ is in you, the body is dead because of sin, but the Spirit is life because of righteousness. But if the Spirit of Him who raised Jesus from the dead dwells in you, He who raised Christ from the dead will also give life to your mortal bodies through His Spirit who dwells in you.

The Apostle Paul wants you to understand the importance between the flesh and the spirit. He says Romans 8:12-14 NKJV, "Therefore, brethren, we are debtors-not to the flesh, to live according to the flesh. For if you live according to the flesh you will die; but if by the Spirit you put to death the deeds of the body, you will live. For as many as are led by the Spirit of God, these are sons of God."

The question that I want to pose to you today is: Is there anything that will stop you from going to heaven if you were to die today? They might be sinful habits, or an unforgiving heart, adultery, or a bad attitude. There are so many sins of the flesh that all of them cannot be named. The only thing I can say is to check yourself and if it is not of God, ask Jesus to forgive you of your sins and receive Him today as your Personal Savior. With old habits sometimes, you may not be able to stop instantly. What you need to do is take it to the Lord in prayer as many times as you need to until that habit is broken in the name of Jesus. God wants you in a position to serve Him daily. Sometimes we get so busy with the business of living that we don't take the time to spend time in prayer and studying His word. I always say everyday is a better day when you take a few minutes with God.

I think about the people who died on September 11th, in hurricanes, the tsunami and earthquakes and I say, "Lord, what's next?" Jesus said, "Prepare for Landing." You might not make it through a 9/11 or a hurricane or tsunami or earthquake. You might pass away in a hospital room, in your own home, on your job. But, I want you to know that when you do leave this earthly journey, and you have prepared for landing, you can meet me on the other side.

Prepare For Landing, Destination Heaven!

About The Author

Arlena D. Lee truly believes that every day is a better day when you take a few minutes with God. She holds a Bachelor of Science in Chemistry from Bethune Cookman University located in Daytona Beach, FL and a Master of Practical Theology from Oral Roberts University which is located in Tulsa, Oklahoma. After being called into the Ministry, she has devoted her time to preaching the gospel, visiting the sick and praying for the lost. Her radio show *"A Few Minutes With God"* inspired most of the sermons in this book, sermons which have become dear to her heart. This book was birthed because of her desire to touch more lives with the gospel. She resides in Ft. Pierce, FL.

www.ingramcontent.com/pod-product-compliance
Lightning Source LLC
Chambersburg PA
CBHW070527010526
44110CB00050B/2193